Blue Murder

'*Blue Murder* is funny, sharp and playful. It's so disruptive it threatens at any time to implode.' *Independent on Sunday*.

Subtitled a play or two, *Blue Murder* opens with *Foreign Bodies*, where Swinging London meets bourgeois Shrewsbury and the drinks are laced with cyanide. As the son of the household struggles to write his first play, a murder story is offered to him on a plate. The second half, *A Game of Soldiers*, is a Whitehall farce taking place in St James's Palace. The same dramatist has brought his complete play to be censored but the Lord Chamberlain's Men have a few shameful secrets of their own to hide, including a priapic guardsman.

Peter Nichols was born in Bristol in 1927 and educated there at the Grammar School and Old Vic Theatre School. After National Service in India, Malaya and Hong Kong, he was an actor in repertory and television for five years, then a teacher in London schools. He has written some twenty original plays and adaptations for television, six feature films and the following stage plays: *A Day in the Death of Joe Egg, The National Health, Forget-Me-Not Lane, The Freeway, Chez Nous, Privates on Parade, Born in the Gardens, Passion Play, Poppy* and *A Piece of My Mind*. These have won four *Evening Standard* Awards, a Society of West End Theatres Award for Best Comedy and two Best Musical Awards. He was resident playwright at the Guthrie Theatre, Minneapolis, where he co-directed *The National Health*. He has also directed revivals of *Joe Egg* and *Forget-Me-Not Lane* at Greenwich and the first production of *Born in the Gardens* at Bristol. The 1985 Broadway revival of *Joe Egg* won two Tonys. *Feeling You're Behind*, a book of memoirs, came out in 1984.

By the same author

Plays
A Day in the Death of Joe Egg
The National Health (or Nurse Norton's Affair)
Forget-Me-Not Lane
Chez Nous
The Freeway
Privates on Parade
Born in the Gardens
Passion Play
Poppy
A Piece of My Mind
Plays: One (A Day in the Death of Joe Egg, The National Health, Forget-Me-Not Lane, Hearts and Flowers, The Freeway)
Plays: Two (Chez Nous, Privates on Parade, Born in the Gardens, Passion Play, Poppy)

Autobiography
Feeling You're Behind

PETER NICHOLS

Blue Murder

a play or two

Methuen Drama

A Methuen Modern Play

First published in Great Britain in 1996
by Methuen Drama
an imprint of Reed International Books Ltd
Michelin House, 81 Fulham Road, London SW3 6RB
and Auckland, Melbourne, Singapore and Toronto
and distributed in the United States of America
by Heinemann, a division of Reed Elsevier Inc.
361 Hanover street, Portsmouth, New Hampshire
NH 03801 3959

ISBN 0 413 71420 9

A CIP catalogue record for this book is available from the British Library

Typeset by Wilmaset Ltd, Birkenhead, Wirral
Printed in Great Britain by Cox & Wyman Ltd, Reading, Berkshire

Blue Murder

Blue Murder was first presented at Quakers Friars, Bristol, by Show of Strength on 1 November 1995. The cast was as follows:

Hester/Daphne	Pat Rossiter
Edwin/Trimmer	Alan Moore
Colin/Nick	Sam Bond
Isabel/Prue	Claudia McNulty
Lionel/Parrott	Andrew Hilton
Bernie/Randy	Meredith Davies
Rex/Denis/Jack	Kevin Kibbey

It was restaged for a national tour by the Touring Partnership in September 1996. The cast was as follows:

Hester/Daphne	Nichola McAuliffe
Edwin/Trimmer	Barry Foster
Colin/Nick	Matthew Lloyd Davies
Isabel/Prue	Ysobel Gonzalez
Lionel/Parrott	Anton Rodgers
Bernie/Randy	Ian Reddington
Rex/Denis/Jack	Andrew Harrison

For both productions:
Director Peter Nichols
Associate Director Alan Coveney
Designer Andrea Montag

An oblique sign / indicates that this is where the next speech should start, interrupting the first.

ACT ONE

FOREIGN BODIES

Scene One

Two rooms of a substantial, light and pleasant house in the suburbs of Shrewsbury in Shropshire. The time is spring, 1963 but the style is the 1950s.

A small study on audience left, lit from a window on the left which has views of a garden; a door in the upstage wall; wainscoting; a large desk with a telephone in front of the window; a case of cups and trophies; stereo extension speakers against an imaginary wall which would, if it existed, divide the two rooms from each other. A fragment of the missing wall and several other features indicate the limit of each room – carpets, placed furniture, perhaps even a raised level for the study.

The main area's the living-room, also with a door in its upper wall from the passage or hall; in the right wall, which is at an angle, French windows on to the rear garden, of which some should be seen: a paved terrace, trees and flowers in a bed. A baby grand piano, its keyboard hidden; chintz sofas and armchairs; carpets with parquet surrounds; a stereo unit against the imaginary wall beside a chair; large flower arrangements in vases.

The song 'Nice People' is heard before the lights (or tabs) go up. EDWIN's *in the study. He lights a cigar and polishes a trophy, starts to mix drinks for* HESTER *and himself.* HESTER *comes in through the French windows wearing a broad-brimmed straw hat, carrying a trug with fresh-cut flowers and removing gardening gloves. She frowns at the music and calls:*

HESTER. Edwin!

He can't hear, so she turns down the volume on the radiogram. In the study he looks at the speakers, puts the trophy back on its shelf. She shrugs and smiles, removes hat, takes a glass vase that's half full of water and begins arranging her blooms. EDWIN *leaves the study and reappears in the living-room, leaving the study door open to the passage, bringing the drinks.*

EDWIN. Sorry. Was it too loud?

HESTER. Well, we're not deaf. But we shall be if you play your new whatever-it-is at that volume.

EDWIN. Stereo. Hi-fi. I thought you liked that song.

'Nice People with Nice Manners
But got no money at all.'

They dance, singing along with the record.

EDWIN *and* HESTER. 'We've got such nice habits, we keep rabbits
But got no money at all . . .'

HESTER. It is nice, yes. Funny too. People pretending to be what they're not.

EDWIN. Missing the news.

He stops the record and tunes the radio, catching snatches of speech and music, including an early Beatles.

HESTER. This is Gracious Living.

EDWIN. It is indeed, my dear, thanks to you.

HESTER. Thank you kindly, sir, said she. But I meant these Tall Bearded Irises. It's their name: Gracious Living. And the delphiniums Hilda Lucas are a lovely show this year too.

RADIO NEWSREADER. . . . only a matter of time before Southern Rhodesia also gains its independence. Solicitors acting for Mr John Profumo, Secretary of State for War, have today begun an action for damages against the Italian and French newspapers *Il Tempo* and *Paris-Match* which have thrown doubt on the minister's statement to the House in which he denied impropriety with Miss Christine Keeler.

EDWIN. Good for him!

RADIO. Mr MacMillan the Prime Minister has repeated that his faith in Mr Profumo remains unshaken and regards the matter as closed. This afternoon Mr and Mrs Profumo went to the races with the Queen Mother.

HESTER. Oh, that's nice.

EDWIN (*turning it down*). You see, the mistake the French and Italians make is judging our ministers by their own. This island hasn't been invaded for a thousand years. Time in which to breed a very different sort of animal.

HESTER. Isn't that how long it takes to grow a nice lawn?

With a gay laugh, ISABEL *and* COLIN *come from the garden, dressed for tennis and carrying rackets.*

COLIN. I'm afraid she's far too good for me.

EDWIN *holds up a warning hand and turns up the volume.*

RADIO. Mr Harold Wilson, new leader of the Labour Party after the unexpected and mysterious death of Mr Hugh Gaitskell, pledged today to lead the party to victory in the next election.

EDWIN. I don't think.

RADIO. Next month he goes to America for meetings with President Kennedy –

EDWIN (*turning off*). And a fat lot of good that will do. Not even Prime Minister and hardly likely to be.

COLIN. More gems from the *Daily Telegraph*.

Makes a wary, sophisticated gesture at ISABEL *behind* EDWIN*'s back.*

HESTER. So, Isabel, did you give my son a good thrashing?

ISABEL. Sorry?

EDWIN. Did you thrash him? Trounce him?

ISABEL. Ah. Hardly. Only took the final set 8–6 after going to seven deuces.

COLIN. So what's the latest on Profumo?

EDWIN. The PM says it's all my-eye-and-Betty-Martin and I'd

sooner believe him than a crew of muck-raking Eyeties and Dagoes.

COLIN. MacMillan's a joke. A dinosaur.

EDWIN. The British people will never want to be led by someone with a funny accent.

COLIN. MacMillan? I agree. They'll kick him out.

EDWIN. Don't try to be funny. You're not half bright enough.

HESTER. For Heaven's sake, you two. I shouldn't be surprised if Colin's right about that girl. There's no smoke without fire.

EDWIN. Ministers don't lie to the House.

COLIN. What!?

HESTER. Please don't raise your voice.

ISABEL. Colin's an actor. He's done Voice Production.

EDWIN. Well, this isn't the working-men's hall or wherever it is you put your shows on.

HESTER. I only know that what with the radio and you, my head's splitting, Edwin, why don't you get us all a nice drink? Mine's a nice G and T.

She downs her drink. EDWIN *frowns.*

EDWIN. Right-oh. Isabel?

ISABEL. Just a lime juice, please. With ice.

EDWIN. Sure? Nothing stronger? And Laurence Olivier?

COLIN. A Scotch, thanks.

ISABEL. I'll just go and change.

She follows EDWIN. HESTER *has done her flowers and now plumps cushions.* EDWIN *enters the study and* ISABEL*'s in the doorway.*

EDWIN. Might as well take yours up, my dear.

ISABEL. Thanks, Mr Boswell.

EDWIN. Shut the door behind you.

She does. He pours it and gives it to her. She sips and waits.

HESTER. She's a really nice girl, dear.

COLIN. D'you think so, Mum? I'm glad because I do too.

She takes a cigarette from the box he offers. They light up. He goes to the piano and doodles chords and boogie rhythms while HESTER *sits on the sofa.*

EDWIN. Twenty-five, didn't you say?

ISABEL. Oh, what for?

EDWIN. Can't have you owing the rent, can we?

ISABEL. Well, thank you, Mr Boswell.

EDWIN *gives her some banknotes. She counts them.*

I'll pay you back.

EDWIN. No hurry.

ISABEL. Mummy and Daddy would have a fit if they found out.

EDWIN. Then they mustn't. No need for everyone to know everything about everybody, is there? If you follow?

ISABEL. Sorry?

EDWIN. Mum's the word. Strictly *entre nous*. Between these four walls.

ISABEL. Oh, the twenty-five pounds?

EDWIN. What else?

ISABEL. I can't imagine.

EDWIN. Good.

HESTER. And I can't pretend Isabel's not a relief after some of the others you brought home.

EDWIN. Stumm, eh? Nuff sed. No comment.

COLIN. Now, now, Mum.

ISABEL. What the eye doesn't see ...

EDWIN. A nod's as good as a wink to a blind horse ...

She taps her nose and goes. He wipes his face, mixes drinks.

HESTER. That fräulein – who was it? –

COLIN. Heidi? Oh, come on, the war's been over nearly twenty years.

HESTER. No, in fact I found her very interesting to talk to. For instance, when she told us the death-camps were all Jewish propaganda.

COLIN. No, Mum, that was rubbish. She was just repeating what her father said.

HESTER. Well, I dare say he'd have known.

COLIN. He was a Nazi.

HESTER. Dad thought she had a point. And he knew a good few Jews before he moved from London. Forever moaning, he said. They're still not welcome in the golf club.

COLIN. Jesus Christ!

HESTER. And don't use bad words. It makes my head ache. No, it wouldn't do to get hitched to a German.

COLIN. Who's talking about getting hitched? I'm only twenty-five.

HESTER. And the Welsh girl – Bronwen? The forward one.

COLIN. You mean tarty?

HESTER. I didn't say that. Only I'm glad you dropped her too.

COLIN. She dropped me.

HESTER. Then she had more sense than I thought. They may seem like us because they speak a sort-of English but they're really not.

COLIN. This is Shrewsbury! We're not ten miles from the Welsh border!

HESTER. The North Welsh aren't so bad. But didn't Bronwen come from the valleys? The coal-mining part?

COLIN. Christ Almighty!

With a cry of rage, he slams down the lid of the keyboard as EDWIN *returns with drinks on tray.*

EDWIN. Bad language again? Any more, you'll feel the back of my hand, big as you are. Just you apologise.

COLIN. Sorry, Mum.

HESTER. Give Mummy a kiss.

He does. EDWIN *gives them their drinks.*

I was only trying to tell him how nice Isabel seems after his other girls. Not at all brassy.

EDWIN. Not like Bronwen. She was a handful, I'd say, son? If you follow me?

He makes handful gestures behind HESTER*'s back.*

HESTER. No need to be coarse, Edwin.

EDWIN. No, but I mean there was plenty of her. Not one of your skin-and-bone Jean Shrimpton girls. Not plump by any means but/ well-covered and not ashamed of it.

HESTER. Yes, I think we take your point.

EDWIN. Whereas Isabel –

HESTER. Is modest, innocent, nicely brought up but without much idea of the wicked world. A sweet English rose.

EDWIN. Sounds more like a blushing violet, eh, boy?

HESTER. She's going to need protecting. Whoever she marries.

EDWIN. Especially in the world you've both chosen. The theatre ... not exactly known for its high moral tone.

COLIN. This isn't the 1890s. It's 1963.

HESTER. I'm surprised her parents let a nice girl take those risks.

EDWIN. Her dad's used to danger. He's a soldier.

HESTER. I thought you said a colonel.

EDWIN. Colonels *are* soldiers.

HESTER. Ah. When I hear the word 'soldier' I always picture privates. I know, if I had a sweet young daughter like that, I'd get no sleep if I thought of her living in – what-do-they-call-them? –

EDWIN. Dressing-rooms?

HESTER. No.

COLIN. Digs?

HESTER. Such a horrid word.

EDWIN. You heard Uncle Lionel talk about the actresses' home, son?

COLIN. There aren't any actresses' homes now! Just ordinary people who let out rooms.

HESTER. Well, you take care of her. That's all I'm saying. She's precious. We very much approve of her, don't we, dear?

EDWIN. Delightful.

HESTER. I so wanted a little girl.

EDWIN. And talking of Brother Lionel, where's he got to?

HESTER. The public library, I think he said, to check his stocks and shares in the paper.

COLIN. Talk about mean! With all that money he's put away, he still won't spend twopence on a *Telegraph*. Quite funny, that.

He takes out a pad and pen and makes the first of many notes. They watch him with interest.

HESTER. When you see the house where he still lives in the East End of London, you can't doubt he's on the tight side.

EDWIN. Brother Lionel, Sister Effie, Brother Walter, Brother Albert and I grew up in a very different world from the one we live in here.

COLIN. Sounds like a monastery.

EDWIN. In a way it was. And I had the gumption to go over the wall. My business brought me here and I married your mother soon after the first war. Whereas they stayed and never changed. Grew old in that gaslit house, still with no power, no hot water, a bath in the kitchen that Sister Effie filled with kettles. An outside convenience and chamber-pots in the bedrooms. Right up to the present day.

HESTER. Oh, not again. The history of London's East End? As though we don't know it off by heart.

COLIN. That's called The Exposition. When a character in a play tells the others what they must already know as a way of telling the audience who don't.

EDWIN. Thanks for the lesson, Bernard Shaw.

ISABEL *returns in twin-set, Gor-ray skirt with pearl necklace.*

HESTER. Ah, my dear, I see your ears are burning.

ISABEL. Perhaps the sun caught them.

HESTER. I mean we've been singing your praises. Come and sit by me.

COLIN *gives her a brief kiss on her cheek.*

EDWIN. Now now, you'll make the old man jealous. Eh, Isabel?

HESTER. For Heaven's sake, Edwin, the poor girl's blushing. Try to forget those Cockney ways you grew up with.

EDWIN. I was going to suggest that after a drink we play a set of mixed doubles.

ISABEL. I've only just got dressed.

EDWIN. And very nice you look ... but not as nice as you did in your whites with the light cotton blouse and those shorts drawn in tight/ at the waist ...

COLIN (*suddenly bursting out*). Jesus Christ Almighty! You're like some dirty old man in Soho. Some old sod in a/ grubby mac!

EDWIN. You'd better wash your mouth out with soap-and-water. But first an apology's/ due to your mother and –

COLIN. Apologise? To you? After all that disgusting innuendo and single *entendre*! You're joking, of course!

He goes, slamming the door.

EDWIN. Then I apologise on his behalf. And I assure you I meant nothing untoward about your shorts and bare calves and thighs/ and I hope you know that ...

HESTER. Yes, very well, Edwin. Why don't you get rid of that vase of Enchantment Lilies and fill it with clean rain-water for me?

EDWIN. The old man's got his marching orders, eh, Isabel?

He takes the flowers off to the garden.

HESTER. They make a nice show. Produced from crossing hybrids of hollandicum and tigrinum.

ISABEL. They're lovely.

HESTER. Lovely but gone over. Edwin hardly touches the garden. Being away so often on his country-house sales. So much cataloguing and auctioning in the stately homes. No picnic being an estate agent. Does your mother do it all at the Mill House?

ISABEL. Mostly. Daddy's usually on the links.

HESTER. My dear, you mustn't take any notice of Colin's dad. Or say anything to Mummy and Daddy about what he said about your tennis clothes. They might not understand.

ISABEL. Understand? Sorry. I don't think I do either.

HESTER *gets up and moves about, fussing with flowers.*

HESTER. No. Why should you? There's nothing *to* understand.

ISABEL. I was glad to get into a skirt and twin-set because I was so embarrassed by these bruises on my thighs. I know Mr Boswell kept looking at them.

HESTER. Only out of sympathy, I'm sure.

ISABEL *lifts the hem of her skirt and shows the bruises.* HESTER *looks closely for some time and* ISABEL *meets her eyes.*

It must have been a nasty fall.

ISABEL. I think in the Scottish Play so many accidents happen because you think they will. You kind-of sort-of almost *will* them. And then of course there's far more chance for them – what with boiling cauldrons and battles and sword-fights and children being killed.

HESTER. Yes ... now which play are we talking about?

ISABEL. The Scottish Play. Shakespeare's tragedy that starts with the witches meeting this/ Scottish lord and –

HESTER. Oh, *Macbeth*!

ISABEL. Oops! That's torn it.

She goes to the hall and reappears in the study. She spits into a potted plant and begins turning on the spot.

We see LIONEL *coming through the front garden; sees* ISABEL *alone in the study, comes to the window for a closer look. He's wearing a tweed cap and raincoat.*

EDWIN *returns with the vase.*

EDWIN. Where's Isabel?

HESTER. She just walked out. What could I have said?

EDWIN. Nothing about the Masons?

HESTER. No. Why?

He shrugs, looks into the hall. HESTER *goes to the garden with her trug.*

ISABEL. Double double toil and trouble
Round the cauldron boil and bubble

LIONEL *continues on the way he was going.*

ISABEL. Save my head from falling rubble.
So say all of us. Amen!

She stops turning but goes on reciting. LIONEL *appears in the door and watches, now without his outdoor clothes. In his sixties, wearing a pre-war dark three-piece suit.*

ISABEL. Oh, Uncle Lionel! You startled me.

LIONEL. Somebody mention the Scottish Play?

ISABEL. 'Fraid so.

LIONEL. They're not in The Business. They don't know.

He takes notes from his wallet.

Twenty-five, didn't you say?

ISABEL. Oh, what for?

LIONEL. Can't have you owing the rent, can we?

ISABEL. Well, thank you, Mr Boswell.

He gives her some banknotes. She counts them.

I'll pay you back.

COLIN *enters living-room, now in casuals.*

LIONEL. No hurry.

ISABEL. Mummy and Daddy would have a fit if they found out.

EDWIN. I'll get your mother a drink.

LIONEL. Then they mustn't.

COLIN. Another? It's such a feeble excuse for going to the study.

LIONEL. No need for everyone to know everything about everybody, is there?

EDWIN. What d'you mean, excuse?

LIONEL. If you follow?

COLIN. Every time some secret meeting happens, 'I'll get your mother a drink.' It's clumsy stagecraft. Why aren't the drinks in here?

ISABEL. I'm sorry?

LIONEL. Mum's the word.

He taps his nose, opens the door, follows her out.

EDWIN. What, and have the place smelling like a four-ale bar?

COLIN. And the telephone? Why no extension in this room? It's the sort of house that would have phones everywhere.

He puzzles over his notebook as ISABEL *and* LIONEL *enter.*

LIONEL. You must never mention the Scottish Play with theatricals. Bad luck.

ISABEL. I had to go to another room to take the curse off.

EDWIN. Wasn't it in that show you sustained those bruises?

ISABEL. A matinée at Nuneaton, yes. I was Lady Macduff backing away from the murderers and went headlong off the rostrum on to a brace cleated to a flat.

She sits, showing the bruises. They look closely.

LIONEL. They're taking a long time to heal.

ISABEL. Oh, gosh. You should have seen them two months ago.

She and COLIN *look at them looking.* EDWIN *breaks away.*

LIONEL. It's *Twelfth Night* you're in together, am I right?

He pokes at his pipe with a cleaner, blows through it noisily.

ISABEL. Yes. I'm Viola and he's my identical twin Sebastian.

EDWIN. This another sample of exhibition, son? Telling us what we already know/ so as to tell the audience –

COLIN. Exposition.

ISABEL. Viola dresses as a boy and a woman falls for her. All very AC/DC. You know, Mr Boswell?

LIONEL. Sebastian's not much of a part, as I recall?

COLIN. Let's face it, acting's only a sideline for me. A way of earning a living while I write my plays.

LIONEL (*with a gruff bark of a laugh*). Writing now, is it?

EDWIN. No reason you shouldn't stay home and work for me at the auction rooms, write in your spare time. Or get a nice job with the Civil Service.

COLIN. I have. I'm working for the Arts Council.

He and ISABEL *laugh and he kisses her. The elders watch.*

LIONEL. Talking of playwrights, Somerset Maugham.

He lights his pipe and blows a cloud of smoke.

He makes a decent screw. Heard one of his last week on the Rediffusion. Bit broad for Sister Effie. She went off to bed. She thought it was going to be nice, she said, but it turned out unnecessary.

COLIN*'s busy writing this down.*

She wanted to wash out his mouth with Lysol. I said she'd never get the chance, seeing he lived on the Riviera. 'Don't know where that is,' she said, 'never been there, never been asked.

HESTER *returns, carrying more flowers, which she puts in the waiting vase.*

LIONEL }
EDWIN } 'Wouldn't go if I was.'

EDWIN *looks uneasy whenever* LIONEL *reminds him of his origins.*

HESTER. I hope we're not on the subject of London's East End again? Really, Lionel, I don't know how you've stood it all these years.

EDWIN. Hardly ever there, are you? More often up the West End.

HESTER. Yes, Isabel, auditioning actresses.

COLIN. Actresses!

HESTER. And playing while they sing.

ISABEL. Really?

HESTER. Did you ever find yourself up in Lionel's eyrie, my dear?

COLIN. Hardly. She's not a chorus-girl. Or contortionist.

HESTER. My brother-in-law could have been a professional concert pianist if he'd wanted.

LIONEL. What? And wind up selling matches? Or in the drunkards' home. Sleeping over a rope in the doss-house. No fear.

COLIN. What was it you called the actresses' hostel, Uncle?

LIONEL. The Cats' Home. Or Billingsgate. The Fish Market.

He laughs. COLIN *makes a note.* HESTER *puts the vase in the 'fireplace', down centre.*

HESTER. There. Begonia Evansiana.

LIONEL. What's the boy writing down?

HESTER. Edwin, where are those drinks? And Lionel, why don't you and I raise the tone somewhat with a nice song?

EDWIN *goes into the study and mixes more drinks,* HESTER *and* LIONEL *to the piano to look through sheet music. He plays and she sings first lines and phrases.* COLIN *leads* ISABEL *downstage.*

COLIN. I'm going to ask Dad for that money you need.

ISABEL. No, don't. Please. I couldn't look him in the face.

COLIN. I won't tell him what it's for. I'll say I've got to get my dinner-jacket from the pawnbroker's. It's required by the Equity contract anyway.

ISABEL. As long as you don't say it's for me ... my rent arrears. I must show Mummy and Daddy I can manage on what I earn. They'd jump at the chance to have me back at the Mill House, you know that ... to keep me from The Stage ... fix me up with a nice Young Conservative.

COLIN (*writing again*). Let's face it, Theatre's so drearily respectable now and our parents still think it's vagabonds and gypsies and the four-ale bar. Grotesque. I can use it in the scene where the young actor son comes home/ with his girlfriend ...

ISABEL. Darling, nothing must cause trouble with your people. Or between us. Far rather give up the stage than that, because I love you so very much.

She takes his hand and kisses it, unseen by the others.

COLIN. I can't afford to be in love. Can't afford to be in anyone else's power.

ISABEL. Oh, how could you be? I'd never hurt you, my darling.

LIONEL (*seeing them kiss*). That's enough of that, you two. My little sister would describe that in one word with a capital S ... for Smutty.

HESTER. I'm sure she would. But we're not in Stepney now. Ah, yes. 'My Hero' from 'The Chocolate Soldier'.

COLIN. Do me a favour, Mum ...

ISABEL. Oh, no, I love that song, Mrs Boswell.

COLIN. This is the age of Elvis Presley. The Beatles. It's not 1890, it's 1963. No, he's already said that.

ISABEL. Who?

COLIN (*making a note*). Colin.

ISABEL. You.

COLIN (*with a nervous glance out front*). Yes.

HESTER *sings and* ISABEL *joins in as* LIONEL *plays.*

HESTER. Come, come, I love you only
My heart is true.
Come, come, my life is lonely
I long for you.

EDWIN *returns with drinks on tray, hands them out, sings too.*

Come, come, naught can efface you,
My arms are aching now to embrace you ...

'Nice People' rises to drown their singing as the lights go.

Scene Two

During which the daylight outside turns to dusk. COLIN *and* ISABEL *are singing 'A Coupla Swells'.* HESTER *and* EDWIN *sit listening.* LIONEL *accompanies with accuracy but not much verve.* ISABEL *and* COLIN *try to swing, with plenty of practised choreography, using tennis rackets as props.*

ISABEL *and* COLIN. We're a coupla sports,
The pride of the tennis-courts.
In June, July and August we look cute
when we're dressed in shorts.

COLIN *breaks out of the act.*

COLIN. Et cetera, et cetera, blah, blah, blah ...

HESTER. Oh, I was enjoying that.

COLIN. Not your fault, Uncle. We hadn't rehearsed together, that's all. There was no rhythm to it, no swing. It's not Beethoven.

LIONEL. I rather gathered so.

ISABEL. You're always so critical. Such a perfectionist!

LIONEL. All mouth and no trousers, eh, Isabel?

EDWIN *and* LIONEL *laugh.*

COLIN. Shut up, shut up, shut up! You're – unspeakable grotesques! Let's face it.

EDWIN. You'll feel the back of my hand/ in a minute –

COLIN. No, I shan't. Because I'm twenty-five and you're sixty ... doddering towards the pension you've given up your whole life/ to earn ...

EDWIN. Hush-a-mouth, sonny. Hush-a-mouth!

He taps COLIN*'s lips with his finger and dances away.*

Let someone talk who's got something to say for himself, eh, Isabel?

HESTER. Edwin, try not to behave like a Cockney. Why don't you get us another drink?

EDWIN. You've only just had one.

HESTER (*looking at her empty glass*). Have I?

EDWIN. And now it's my turn to provide the entertainment. Lionel, you remember 'Ikey on the telephone'?

LIONEL *at once plays an arpeggio introduction.*

COLIN. God!

EDWIN. And don't take the Lord's name in vain.

HESTER. Get us a drink, dear.

COLIN *storms out to the study and starts pouring drinks.*

COLIN. I'll kill the old bastard!

EDWIN. You've got to imagine the big nose, Isabel.

LIONEL. One big enough to hang a bunch of keys on.

EDWIN (*adopting stage-Jewish accent and posture*).
Vos you dere, Abie? Vos you dere?
And vos you all alone?
Zis vos Ikey calling on our prand-new telephone.

The front doorbell rings, an electric chime.

Oh, dash it all! Who the dickens is that?

HESTER. It might be Mrs Cartwright about our bring-and-buy for the W.V.S.

EDWIN. We'd better wait, Lionel.

LIONEL *plays a Schubert Impromptu as* HESTER *looks off.*

HESTER. Colin, if it's Mrs Cartwright, ask her to wait in the morning-room.

BERNIE *appears in the study window.*

COLIN. Morning-room!

BERNIE *taps at the window, goes.* COLIN *goes to the front door.*

LIONEL. Are you fond of Schubert, Isabel?

ISABEL. Terribly, yes.

COLIN *returns to the study with* BERNIE*: mid-twenties, boyish, Cockney-smart, longish hair.* HESTER *shuts the door.*

COLIN. What'll you have?

BERNIE. A light ale, thanks.

HESTER. A stranger. No one I know anyway. Perhaps a friend of Colin's.

BERNIE. How long's she been here?

COLIN. Two days. We've got a week out. We're together in a tour/ of Shakespeare's –

BERNIE. Yeah, I know.

COLIN. You do? How?

BERNIE. Ta. Cheers.

EDWIN. If Pipsqueak's dealing with him, I might as well go on with Ikey.

HESTER. If we're having company, I'd sooner Lionel played something nicer.

She stands close to the wall and leans in a listening attitude.

BERNIE. So ... your people aren't short of a few bob then.

COLIN. How'd you know Isabel? How d'you know she'd be here? Who are you? What d'you say your name is?

BERNIE. Nice house. Sodding great garden. Snag is Shrewsbury's some way off the beaten track.

COLIN. Not if you're going to Aberystwyth or Llandudno ...

BERNIE. I rest my case.

EDWIN. Look, shall I get us all another ... ?

HESTER *signals him to shut up. She can't hear through the wall, though she's using an empty tumbler.*

BERNIE. Where is she then?

COLIN *leads him out and into the living-room.*

COLIN. Visitor for you, sweetie.

BERNIE *enters with his beer.* HESTER, *startled, drops the glass, picks it up.* LIONEL *stops playing.*

BERNIE. Hullo, Angel. You're looking good. Shakespeare suits you. But there's more to life than good health, right?

EDWIN. How are you? Are you quite well? Edwin Boswell. My good lady Hester. Brother Lionel.

BERNIE (*shaking hands*). I was saying to whosit here, nice set-up. Garden and all, I see. Tennis court. Grand piano.

LIONEL. *Baby* grand.

BERNIE. Got a pool?

HESTER. A pond. A lily pond.

ISABEL. How did you find me?

BERNIE. Colin's agent. Some journey. Paddington, Rugby, Coventry, Birmingham, Wolverhampton, Kampala, Uganda –

ISABEL. But what for?

BERNIE. Fetch you back. I'm lonely.

ISABEL. Let's go in the garden, shall we, just you/ and me –

COLIN. Just a minute. What d'you mean, fetch her back? Who is he? What's he to you? What are you to him?

BERNIE. Oh, didn't she say?

ISABEL. You bastard. This is my chance to go legit.

BERNIE. I never thought you'd stick it. Reckoned you'd be back inside a fortnight.

COLIN. Legit? She's already legit. She toured in *Macbeth* ... didn't you?

LIONEL. Oops! That name again. Now she'll have to go outside, turn round three times,/ recite the charm –

HESTER. Whatever for?

ISABEL. Well, my bad luck's come anyway. And it's not *Macbeth*. It's Bernie Morgan.

She looks at her glass.

Can I have something stronger? A Bloody Mary?

HESTER. I think we all need another, dear.

EDWIN. But I want to hear what this is/ all about –

HESTER. The quicker you get them, the sooner you'll be back.

EDWIN *goes to the study where he pours fast like a barman.*

BERNIE. *Macbeth*? That what you told them? What as, one of the bleeding witches? No. Nearest she got to the classics till now was playing a slave of the occult in the movie *Black Magic*.

COLIN. Don't remember seeing that. (*To* ISABEL.) So you've been in films? (*When she doesn't answer, to* BERNIE.) Did it go on general release?

BERNIE. Only Soho. And Europe. Made a bomb in Denmark. I can't bear to look at it now. Crude. Gratuitous. Entirely unmotivated. The visuals just about pass but the sound quality's appalling. This was before my neo-realist phase. I was doing a good deal of Gothic Horror at the time. Nowadays I'm exploring the aesthetics of commercials. A lot of hand-held stuff. Rapid cutting. Know what I mean?

COLIN. Not sure I do, no. Hand-held what exactly?

BERNIE. Hand-held cameras. Fabulous. Going to transform movies entirely. Not that our clientèle would notice. Long as they get plenty of tits and arse, leather gear, a climactic sequence involving discipline and punishment, they're easy ... know what I mean? Long as it's laid on thick and fast, they don't give a toss for The Erotic ... you can elbow your slow and subtle arousal ... try a long tease with them they'll be demanding their ackers back. We're not talking about Soft Core. They reckon there's enough of that in their local Odeon. *Tristan and Isolde* they can get at Covent Garden, right? Our punters want the kosher article.

ISABEL. It was a job. I needed work. I'd just arrived in town. I was trying to find my feet.

BERNIE. Hang about. I saved your bacon. You'd just been ditched by/ that randy old bugger brought you up from Great Yarmouth.

ISABEL. Why are you doing this? What have you got to gain?

COLIN. What randy old bugger?

EDWIN *has returned with tray of drinks. Hands them out during a silence.*

EDWIN. Now if you can't refrain from language/ of that sort –

BERNIE. *Black Magic* was the first of a series. She didn't say? They got more explicit as we studied the market. It wasn't just when she was hard up. Come on, Angel, you loved the work. Say you didn't. Your slumbering libido was awakened. Before me they were all butterfingered. You'd learnt nothing. You could have been a virgin. (*Then to* COLIN.) Did you think she still was? (*And when he doesn't answer.*) I suppose you are yourself, are you? (*And to* ISABEL.) D'you think he is? (*And to* COLIN.) I know you are. I know you've only kissed and cuddled.

LIONEL. Do I take it, young woman, you got those bruises on that film?

BERNIE. Things got a touch out-of-hand. Her leading man was a bit of a psychopath, to be quite honest with you.

ISABEL. I didn't notice you calling 'cut!'.

BERNIE. Wouldn't have been much point, the way you two were going at it.

LIONEL. Hell's bells, Colin, you've picked a right one here. And you thinking she was a Shakespearean actress . . .

HESTER. I don't know what you find so amusing, Lionel.

BERNIE. Oh, I do, Mrs Boswell. Only too well. He's looking down his nose and that's the kind of snobbery that keeps this country a mere backwater in the river of European culture. Shakespeare never turned his nose up at violence and cruelty, cannibalism or torture. Look at *Lear*, the Histories, *Titus Andronicus*. And who can deny dominance has been the crucial experience of our times? Dictatorship. Discipline. Then revolution and chaos then again the iron fist. We British led the world in slavery . . . invented the concentration camp. Founded colonies with the lash and gallows. In the works of the great pornographers, a slave's resistance is often a metaphor for revolt, a woman's submission a way of showing perfect love. Even a cursory reading of de Sade raises questions of freedom and captivity we neglect at our peril. It's an emasculated view of art that denies us that dimension.

LIONEL. You've got the gift of the gab, I know that. Swear black was white. And all you are is a smutty little scopophiliac.

HESTER. Whatever they are when they're at home.

EDWIN. Peeping Toms, my love. Presumably.

LIONEL. A word in the right ear you'll find yourself behind bars.

ISABEL. Are you threatening Bernie? Are you?

LIONEL. Not only him. You too. Taking in my nephew, making him look a nana . . . getting yourself invited to his family home. These are people of standing, not to be bothered by scabby tarts and pimps.

HESTER. Really, Lionel.

LIONEL. I beg your pardon, Hester. I call a spade a spade.

ISABEL. Do you?

LIONEL (*to* EDWIN). When the cap fits.

ISABEL. Takes one to know one, eh? You remember me, don't you? I knew you straight off. I'd come to town to get an acting job. Only done the one at Yarmouth. Traipsed up and down the stairs of all the agents round Cambridge Circus. Finished up in yours. Your eyrie, did you call it? I'll drink to that. Bloody weird. Alone with you, auditioning for Christmas panto. 'Now, my dear, which part are you hoping for? A member of the chorus of villagers? (*She stands facing him and touches his cheek.*) Or the Fairy Godmother? (*Touching his chest.*) Or do you aspire to Principal Boy? Prince Charming? Dick Whittington?'

She touches him between the legs. COLIN *makes a note.*

LIONEL. Prove it.

EDWIN. You're not writing that down, boy?

HESTER. So – which part did you get?

ISABEL. Slave of the Lamp.

BERNIE. Not the goose then?

ISABEL. The girls in the Cats' Home told me pantos were mostly cast on his couch. As well as which, the names were passed on to local businessmen wherever they played. So don't you threaten us, 'cause I'd like nothing better than blowing the whistle on you and all those Buffalos and Foresters and Freemasons.

HESTER. Don't be absurd. The Masons are respectability itself, aren't they, Edwin? *And* exclusively male.

ISABEL. You don't have to tell me. Does she?

EDWIN. I haven't the faintest idea what you mean.

ISABEL. Come off it. What was the fifty quid for?

EDWIN *and* LIONEL. Twenty-five.

They look at each other.

ISABEL. We never went to your actual temples. It was more after-hours parties . . . in stately homes . . . castles and manors and dower houses ... between occupants, the contents under dust-sheets ...

HESTER *waits*. EDWIN *appeals to her*.

COLIN. The sort of country houses where you might have stayed three days and nights cataloguing a sale?

LIONEL. You won't believe a tart's word before mine?

ISABEL. I knew him the moment he opened the door when we arrived here. Something in his manner reminded me how he let us in to that party. He didn't know me though. Not for sure. Didn't notice the girls at all. More the chorus-boys. He wore a uniform and mob-cap from one of the maid's bedrooms.

EDWIN. That's where you're wrong, see? I always took my own.

LIONEL. But what's this about Great Yarmouth? Thought your father the colonel lived in Hampshire.

BERNIE. The what? She never knew her old man. No. Brought up in her mother's boarding-house.

HESTER. Would that be Digs?

BERNIE. Where the artistes used to stay. So one thing led to another. Know what I mean? Late at night after the shows. It wasn't only the curtains that came down. She wound up in the chorus on the end of the pier.

COLIN. So that's why you needed the fifty pounds.

BERNIE. Hang about.

COLIN. You're really hard up.

BERNIE. Bitch! Still set on getting rid of it, were you?

ISABEL. I can't afford to give up work long enough to have a kid. I told you.

COLIN. Kid? What kid? Whose kid?

BERNIE. I want her to have it, she doesn't. Why d'you think I wouldn't pay for an operation? I love her, that's why. I want her to be the mother of my child. The first of many.

ISABEL. And give up my career?

BERNIE. Go back after, if you want to. Anyway you'll soon get pissed off with all that blank verse and no action.

ISABEL. That's all you know. (*To the others.*) I told him: no more blue movies. I'm hanging up my gym slip for good. That's what he couldn't stomach.

BERNIE. You and I are made for each other, darling. It's a life sentence. We go together. The eye and the object. Give and take. Master and slave.

He grabs her arm and turns it so that she is forced to the ground. The others watch. She gives several cries of pain. She bites his hand and he lets go. She crawls away.

HESTER. Dear Me! You've upset the hearth.

She straightens the fire-irons. BERNIE licks his fist.

LIONEL. She's a handful. A regular spitfire.

BERNIE. I didn't notice boyfriend rushing to the rescue. Our resident playwright? More interested in watching? Runs in the family, eh?

HESTER. I think it's time you were leaving. There's a London train at six twenty-three. Edwin will call you a taxi/ won't you, dear?

BERNIE. What was the word you used, Uncle? Scopophiliacs? Takes one to know one, eh? Standing shivering on the brink, afraid to get your tootsies wet. Like the whole country in a way.

COLIN. If we're the spectators, what are you?

BERNIE. I don't disown my early movies. Well, a few of the wide-open beaver shots. No, for me they were a means to an end, a first step towards real features. And I believe, when a less hypocritical climate prevails, the sado-erotic will prove a significant cinema genre. I mean, arousal's certainly got more going for it than paralysis, eh? The sort of English acting and writing that's dead from the waist down.

COLIN. How d'you know what my acting's like?

BERNIE. I've seen you. Twice. Went with Angel when you got her a comp. Down at Guildford. *Private Lives ... Ten Little Niggers.*

ISABEL (*as* COLIN *looks at her*). He's right in a way, love. But it's not your fault. What else could you do but suffer nobly and hide your feelings? Like you're doing now? A middle-class boy playing the game, stiff upper lip, suffer in silence.

BERNIE. Same with your plays and stories.

COLIN. You showed him my plays and stories? That I let you have on trust?

ISABEL. I really wanted his opinion. Thought it would help you. I did pass back a few of the points he made. That you seemed to be knocking on doors and running away before you could deliver your message. That you just describe your characters and leave it to us ... when what the people want is to be led. We look to our heroes and stars to take the whip hand. Dominate us. Not stand there being sensitive.

BERNIE. D'you know the Jewish word 'nebbish'? That came to mind when I watched you up there in your monkey-suit. A tailor's dummy. A penguin. No-balls Boswell.

EDWIN. Just watch how you speak to my son.

HESTER. Does anyone want another drink? Same again all round?

She stands, goes and soon reappears in the study.

COLIN. For a so-called director, you don't seem to have much grasp of theatre convention. The plays you saw me –

HESTER *helps herself to a stiff drink and swallows it in one. In agitation she goes to the window and gazes out at the front garden.* COLIN *walks about while the rest listen.*

– were Naturalistic. I take it you know the term? A recent but even now obsolescent dramatic practice that tries to represent the surfaces of life in the one art-form that obviously can't. To describe the rooms, clothes, furniture and fittings, the way people *seem* to behave. When Natural-ism began a hundred years ago it was a revelation, a purgative reform.

HESTER *purposefully pours drinks for them all.*

But seeing anew always scandalises the lazy mind so audiences cried out in alarm when actors for the first time turned their backs on them, lit cigarettes, read newspapers. Suddenly the people on stage weren't helpless victims jerked about on strings by cruel gods but modern spirits moved by the need to keep a job or feed a family. They reflected the people out there. Of course, the actors can't let on in any way they're aware of being watched. They mustn't talk to them or whisper an aside. There's an invisible wall between. If you aren't playing a dominant character, you don't dominate. In the plays you saw I wasn't Der Führer in a brown shirt but a solicitor in a D.J. Passion wasn't on the agenda. I had to play as cast.

HESTER *fetches a hidden key, opens a desk drawer and takes out a box and from that a glass phial of colourless fluid.*

BERNIE. Yeah, fine, you may have/ had to act like that –

COLIN (*loud and firm*). Which meant to open doors into three-sided rooms and switch on lights and fires controlled by someone in the prompt corner.

He now uses the set he's in to describe these features.

To pass from painted gardens through French windows carrying paper flowers into rooms such as few in the audience have ever seen, leave alone lived in. Three-walled rooms –

They all stare out front as he moves to press his hands against the fourth wall.

– and the most we know about the fourth would be fenders and irons to suggest a fireplace.

He warms his hands above them. HESTER *pours the contents of the phial into the tumbler of beer intended for* BERNIE. COLIN *moves to the dividing 'wall'.*

If the plot requires two rooms, we must pretend there's a wall between and we can't see what's being done a few feet away, however important to the plot.

HESTER *stirs it well and it foams for some moments then she leaves the study with the tray.*

Arrivals and departures must appear accidental and pianos play only when touched, even though the real pianist is in the wings doing it for the actor onstage who can't ...

He runs his fingers up the keys.

ISABEL. – or these days more often on tape to save paying a musician –

HESTER *returns.* EDWIN *helps her with the drinks.*

BERNIE. Granted you may have to *act* it but why go on writing what you've just booted up the arse??

HESTER. Oh, really! Can't you say b.t.m.?

ISABEL. Which, in any case, survives mainly in the English-speaking world. Elsewhere there's been Pirandello and Beckett and Brecht –

COLIN. I know all that.

ISABEL. Right. It was you who taught me. But knowing all this, you still can't break free.

HESTER. You were happy enough to stay here, use our tennis court, pluck our blooms, lie on our lawns. And I don't believe it was a purely mercenary longing. You aspired. You *wanted* to be part of our world.

BERNIE. It's your world's killing your son. Stifling any gift he's got. Break away, man. This is death.

EDWIN. I've told you what to do, son. Stay here, take a partnership in the firm, act with the local SODS and write your plays in your spare time.

HESTER. A beer for you, wasn't it?

Gives BERNIE *his glass.*

LIONEL. There's a lot to be said for the double-life. I've shared a gaslit house in Stepney with Sister Effie while all those years up West ... you can do as you please so long as no one knows.

EDWIN. You let everything 'hang out', where's the suspense?

ISABEL. You've never allowed your feelings to speak, perhaps even to yourself. So hemmed-in, uptight and English.

She caresses him fondly.

COLIN. Oh, I wanted to make love to you but you seemed so pure and defenceless and anyway –

ISABEL. You weren't sure how.

COLIN. Why didn't you teach me?

ISABEL. I was afraid you'd be shocked and run away.

COLIN. We could have brought the two worlds together. Discipline and freedom, like Bernie says. I had nothing to write *about*. We none of us had. Fake rooms with second-hand emotions. With you to teach me, I might have made real things happen in pretend rooms.

BERNIE. Sounds all right. If you ever achieve that kind of stylistic fusion, get in touch. We could maybe work together. But, whether Isabel ever meant to join your family or not, she's blown it now. So – how about you and me trying to make that train you mentioned?

Their embraces have become passionate. BERNIE *waits.*

Angel?

ISABEL. Where's the fire? I'm well in here, knowing all I do. Nobody's about to kick me out. What have I got to go back to with you? A bed-sitting-room in Kentish Town . . . a shilling-in-the-meter gas-fire . . . a public phone on the landing . . . bring up a kid in tat like that? You got to be joking.

COLIN. Yes, please stay.

BERNIE. We'll move. I promise.

ISABEL. Again?

BERNIE. I swear.

ISABEL. For fuck's sake, leave me in peace. How can I choose? I want the best of both your worlds.

She goes upstairs.

BERNIE. Well, if she wants to stay a few days, why not?

EDWIN. I'll call you a cab.

BERNIE. Hang about. I'm staying too. This lady wouldn't want all this reaching the W.V.S. Would you, love?

EDWIN *goes, unnoticed, reappears in study, shuts door.*

HESTER. I'm sure we can discuss it in a civilised fashion over a drink. Ah, you haven't touched your last. Here it is.

BERNIE. Your very good health.

HESTER. Cheers.

EDWIN*'s dialled a number.*

EDWIN. Edwin Boswell for Inspector Crozier, please.

BERNIE *has only drunk a few mouthfuls of his beer when he drops the glass, clutches his throat and falls in a spasm.*

HESTER. Oh, not all over my carpet.

EDWIN. Rex, I've got an interesting couple of characters here I thought you should meet. I'll say no more pro tem. I think you'll get their measure pretty sharpish. And the sun's well over the yard-arm so on the way home why don't you . . . fine . . . see you soon . . .

Puts phone down. BERNIE *lies still.* LIONEL *feels his pulse.*

HESTER. Solution of cyanide. Prussic acid. Edwin always keeps some in his desk.

COLIN. What for?

HESTER. As an antiseptic. Against foreign bodies.

LIONEL. Seems to work.

HESTER. Good riddance.

EDWIN *leaves the study.*

COLIN. But why – ?

HESTER. Ours is a nice part of the world, dear, but – delicate, fragile . . . unwanted weeds must go on the compost heap –

EDWIN (*entering*). The cab will be here in half an hour. Apparently they're all on jobs. What's up with him?

LIONEL. He did as Hester told him. Tasted his last drink.

HESTER. Just smell those night-scented stocks. It's going to be a fine evening.

A lightning flash in the garden. A crash of thunder.

Though it does seem to be clouding over.

She goes out to the twilit garden.

COLIN. She says it was your cyanide.

EDWIN. No need to go that far. I'd called the police. They'd have seen them off.

LIONEL. I'm not so sure. Last thing I wanted was him tittle-tattling around town, all those smutty yarns about the agency . . . not to mention the country parties.

EDWIN. Nobody would have credited them.

COLIN. So aren't they true?

EDWIN *and* LIONEL *laugh.*

LIONEL. No more true than the Minister of War and Lord Astor swimming with tarts in their birthday suits.

EDWIN. But your uncle's right, son. This is a time when every lie can be given credence. Your mother may have acted hastily but –

HESTER *reappears pushing a wheelbarrow laden with a garden fork, spades, boots and gloves. Leaves it close to* BERNIE.

HESTER. There's a perfect spot beneath the Liriodendron. (*Looking back.*) Oh, dear, the carpet!

She goes off to the hall while the men lift BERNIE *into the barrow.* LIONEL *takes the tools while* COLIN *pushes and* EDWIN *steadies the load.*

A reprise of 'Nice People' and the lights go.

Scene Three

HESTER, *vacuuming the carpet where she rolled the barrow, sings along with the tune, continuing when the music fades.* ISABEL *comes in from upstairs, now dressed for cocktails.*

ISABEL. Mrs Boswell –

HESTER. Oh, you startled me.

She switches off the cleaner and disconnects it.

ISABEL. I've been trying to make my mind up.

HESTER. Between the devil and the deep blue sea?

ISABEL. I packed my case once. And unpacked it again. So where's Bernie?

HESTER. Oh, your friend. He's gone.

ISABEL. Gone?

HESTER. On the six twenty-three. There's another in an hour but I'm afraid that's a stopping train ... Wellington, Shifnal,/ Sandwell-and-Dudley –

ISABEL. He left just like that?

HESTER. He said he didn't want to miss it. And as you were a long time gone,/ he must have assumed –

ISABEL. He didn't even call out. Did he leave a message?

HESTER. Perhaps with one of the men. I've been in the garden. Dead-heading.

ISABEL. So where are they?

HESTER. Now? Mulching beneath the Aureomarginatum. The Tulip Tree. Digging in some organic fertiliser. How much land was there at your mother's boarding-house?

ISABEL. A stone yard with a mangle in it.

HESTER. Then you won't know the work a large garden demands. They don't happen naturally. They need feeding, watering, yes, but mostly controlling. Pruning, cutting back, getting rid of pests and blight. But, Isabel, my dear, if you aid and abet Mother Nature, she will work with you, hand-in-hand.

They look out into the garden.

There won't be that many surprises. A rose will never turn into a ficus elastica, no acorn become a Wellingtonia. All will bud and blossom and die in their due season.

ISABEL. Just look at them all digging away. I wondered what they were doing when I looked from the bathroom window, the one with the rear-facing view but not ...

HESTER. Pests are an everlasting threat. The wolves and bears may have gone but we've still got slugs and snails, mice and lice, bugs and slugs ... moles undermining lawns –

ISABEL. Aren't they part of Nature too?

HESTER. Did I say Nature or the *appearance* of Nature. Shall we get ourselves a drink?

She leads the way to the study. ISABEL *follows.*

ISABEL. Not Nature then but Natural-ism? Like Colin said.

HESTER. All over the world they're known as English gardens. Informal, like our lovely countryside itself. The hedgerows and patchwork fields ... Oh, it may sound dull and predictable to you with your exciting city life but consider the consolations. Was yours a Bloody Mary?

ISABEL. Thanks. You mean like peace and quiet ... security ... order? Yeah ... I could do with a bit of that.

HESTER. Everyone could. It's only human nature ... heart's ease ... dreams come true ... mon repos ... Dunroamin.

While ISABEL *looks into the front garden,* HESTER *adds cyanide.*

ISABEL. It's also human nature to crave the jungle ... wild beasts and hairy arms ... a sudden pounce and kill ... the taste of blood ...

HESTER *offers the drink and drinks herself.*

What keeps *you* alive?

HESTER. Sometimes in gardens one can kill two birds with one stone ... fertilise and prune. I won't use chemical manures. Everything organic. Bone marrow. Have you seen the Morus Nigra? Commonly known as the Black Mulberry.

ISABEL. Out here?

HESTER. In the front garden, where anyone could have seen? Hardly. We planted ours one late autumn afternoon, many years ago now, soon after a young stranger came to call. Edwin and he were closeted some time together in his study, talking business. Afterwards he too had to make a hasty exit. Like your friend. But in summer the fruit of that tree is luscious.

ISABEL*'s now sitting on the desk.* HESTER *touches her cheek, then her breasts.* ISABEL *doesn't move. Thunder as* COLIN *comes from the garden, changes wellingtons for shoes. He winds up the lead and takes the cleaner off.*

ISABEL *allows* HESTER *to embrace and kiss her thighs, smiling as she raises her Bloody Mary to drink.* HESTER *sees and stops her, takes the glass, returns it to the tray and pours another.* COLIN *returns to the living-room.*

COLIN. Mum! Isabel!

ISABEL *is being kissed by* HESTER*; at* COLIN*'s call, she goes by the door.* HESTER *remains, drinking her gin as* ISABEL *enters the living-room.*

ISABEL. Don't look at me. I'm hideous. I cried myself nearly to sleep up there. My eyes are all swollen.

COLIN. I wish I'd known. I love to see you cry. Makes me feel so masterful. But why?

ISABEL. All the trouble I've caused you and your family. The things I said about your father and uncle.

COLIN. You made them sound really interesting for the first time. Both dirty old men and my dad a paederast to boot. The Masons not just a gang of grocers with rolled-up trousers but a crossroads in the white slave traffic.

HESTER *in the study pours drinks, singing snatches of operetta.*

And you – not a prissy English rose but a full-blown Bougainvillea.

They are on the sofa and he starts making love.

Christ, Uncle was right. I was a nana, with all my talk about art and the future! Going just so far every time because I was afraid to go further and yet nearly fainting to have you.

ISABEL. Nearly? One night you really did. In that cinema. I was so embarrassed. The manager and everything.

COLIN. And all the time you were ... you could have ... teach me now. Please.

She's on top, undoing his trousers. The piano starts playing Schubert, as before. They both look towards the sound booth. COLIN *tries to run to it but his trousers fall round his ankles and bring him down.* ISABEL *dashes across to sit on the stool and mime along. Almost at once the music stops. She stands and tentatively moves away when it starts again and now* COLIN *sits and plays.*

I can take Bernie's place in your life. You can have the best of both worlds. Security and danger. Some ways I wish he hadn't gone. I'd like to have worked with him. His gutter know-how may be what my plays need.

The piano stops so he gets up then embraces her again.

ISABEL. But will your people want me here after all that's happened, all they know about me? All I know about them?

COLIN. We'll put it to them. Dad and Uncle anyway. Mum's too pissed to care.

HESTER *with a full tray moves towards the 'wall' and through it to the other room.*

HESTER. Ooops. Sorry.

She turns round and goes back and out of the study door. ISABEL *and* COLIN *are corpsed.*

EDWIN *and* LIONEL *come from the garden, wiping foreheads and hands, changing boots for shoes as* HESTER *enters.*

I say, you two! Good timing. You must have heard a bell ring.

A telephone rings. They glance at the prompt corner. It rings again. HESTER *stands with the tray, bewildered.* COLIN *goes via two doors to the study and answers.*

COLIN. Hullo? . . . I think you must have the wrong number.

Puts it down, glares at the prompt corner. ISABEL *stifles her laughter.* EDWIN *passes the drinks around. Every surface is by now covered by emptied glasses.*

EDWIN. Did you mix these drinks, my dear?

HESTER. I think so.

EDWIN. Not one of your stiff ones, I hope?

COLIN *comes into the room.*

You've been known to serve pretty potent concoctions.

COLIN. Only cold tea and coloured water, eh, Mum?

HESTER. Pardon?

ISABEL. It's what they use in plays. To look like wine and whisky.

COLIN. Otherwise the actors would be drunk.

HESTER. Ah!

Tries to sit gracefully but collapses into the sofa. The piano starts playing. LIONEL, *standing by it, quickly sits and mimes.*

LIONEL. Perhaps we can all have another song before you catch your train, young woman?

Music stops.

COLIN. She's *not* going.

EDWIN. Who says?

COLIN (*going on to his knees to her*). I do.

LIONEL. And what about her? You broached it, have you?

COLIN. She's going to be one of the family.

EDWIN. She's certainly in the family *way*.

COLIN (*head against her belly*). Ah, yes.

LIONEL. She says.

ISABEL. In six months, if we don't take steps, I'll be having Bernie's baby.

COLIN. And I'm prepared to be the father.

EDWIN. Of course you'll have to get married pronto. Make it all above board.

LIONEL. Then your interests would be ours.

COLIN. You'd be part of the family.

ISABEL. I'd want the terms to be drafted so that should either party infringe a clause, the dispute would go to arbitration. We should all know what's expected.

LIONEL. Of you? You wouldn't knob it.

ISABEL. Of all of you.

COLIN. To teach me all you know.

LIONEL. And keep your hand in with the odd performance.

ISABEL. Odd occasional? Or odd peculiar?

LIONEL *and* EDWIN *laugh.*
COLIN'*s hands are exploring her body. She takes one and bites his fingers, making him flinch.*

COLIN. Oh, yes.

LIONEL, EDWIN *and* HESTER *watch.* ISABEL *considers* COLIN, *caresses his hair, then shakes her head and moves to the French windows. She stands looking into the garden.*

ISABEL. I'll miss him though, the randy bastard.

EDWIN. Now listen here, I'm only giving the idea house-room because young Mary Ann here has got the hots for you. I'm not arguing the toss. Take it or leave it.

LIONEL. Steady, Ted.

ISABEL. Hang about. Who's holding the trumps here?

EDWIN. All those smutty stories, that's your word against ours.

LIONEL. Both parties would have to keep stumm about the other.

ISABEL. Those evergreens, what d'you call them, Hester?

HESTER. Cupressus Lawsoniana.

ISABEL. Don't they form a perfect screen from the neighbours!

COLIN, EDWIN *and* LIONEL *look at each other.*

HESTER. She saw you from the bathroom mulching the Tulip Tree.

ISABEL. But which is the Black Mulberry you spoke of, darling?

LIONEL. S'welp me Bob.

EDWIN *rounds on* HESTER *who drains her glass. Thunder and lightning reveal* CROZIER *in the front garden. Some see him.*

EDWIN. Ah! That'll be Rex Crozier.

Door chime. REX *runs to the front door, out of sight.*

COLIN. *Inspector* Crozier?

EDWIN. I asked him to drop by.

ISABEL (*confused*). You called the police?

EDWIN. Before any of this happened.

Door chimes again.

HESTER. Why doesn't someone answer the door?

Telephone rings.

Phone.

Chimes.

Door.

ISABEL. Yes. You afraid to let him in?

EDWIN *goes.*

LIONEL. Is it a deal then?

ISABEL. Deal? I dictate the terms here.

LIONEL. But in principle?

Thunder and lightning.

HESTER. Whatever's happening to the weather?

EDWIN *ushers* REX *into the study. A stage detective in a mac. He mimes beating rain off his hat, brushing shoulders.*

REX. Dirty night. Threatening.

EDWIN. What's your poison? The usual?

REX. Scotch as it comes, yes. Will you be at the initiation of our new brother next Tuesday?

EDWIN. I should say. I'm his sponsor.

REX. So you are. It slipped my mind. So much slips my mind these days.

HESTER *goes to listen at the 'wall'.*

EDWIN. I wanted a word with you before you meet this girl.

REX. I thought you said there were two? Two suspicious characters?

EDWIN. Just the one.

REX. There's another case, you see. My mind's going. I sometimes think I'll have to take early retirement, Long life!

He raises his glass to EDWIN. *They drink.*

So – one intruder, you say?

EDWIN. An actress pal of my boy.

LIONEL *joins* HESTER *at the wall.*

REX. Actress, eh?

EDWIN. D'you remember the do at Kedlewick Hall?

REX. Remind me.

EDWIN. Turns out she was there. My brother rang his agency this afternoon to check she was on his books. Turned out he'd booked her for *Aladdin* at Wolverhampton. Slave of the Lamp.

REX. It rings a bell.

COLIN *and* ISABEL *join the line at the wall. Door-chime.*

COLIN (*to the prompt corner*). No!

EDWIN. Colin's very soft on her. Wants her for his wife. I think she'd make a man of him frankly. High time too.

REX. Were you beginning to think it ran in the family?

EDWIN. What?

REX. Pillow-biting.

EDWIN. Now, now. I can go either way, you know very well.

REX. That's what they all say. Ambidextrous.

EDWIN. Colin's the living proof. Which is why I'll be glad to see him fixed. She's a lovely girl.

REX. How would you know?

They both laugh.

Well ... this won't get the work done.

EDWIN. You don't mind introducing yourself? I must go upstairs and pluck a sweet pea.

He goes. Not hearing anything, HESTER *finishes her drink and uses the glass to 'listen'.* LIONEL, COLIN *and* ISABEL *follow her lead.*

REX *looks about at the drinks and glasses and sniffs the Bloody Mary mixed by* HESTER. *He pours it into a potted plant and goes, reappearing in the living-room. The plant wilts.*

REX. Hello-hello-hello.

LIONEL, ISABEL *and* COLIN *scatter. He touches* HESTER *who jumps.*

And Hester ... hello. Colin ... and – have we met?

LIONEL. Never!

REX. My mistake. Rex Crozier.

LIONEL. Brother Lionel.

REX. And I don't think we've had the pleasure?

HESTER (*protectively*). Nor likely to. Don't even try.

ISABEL. Isabel Angel.

REX. That the name you go under? For the stage?

ISABEL. No, my real one.

HESTER (*kissing the top of* ISABEL*'s hair*). Angel by name, angelic by nature ...

REX. Haven't I also heard tell an angel in Show Business is someone who puts up money for shows? Someone who's got more money than sense?

LIONEL. Not in every case. It's a reasonable risk.

COLIN. And brings you close to a more exciting world.

REX. Bless my soul, you live and learn. So that someone with a bit to spare might risk a flutter?

ISABEL. Such as Mr Boswell.

HESTER. Where's Edwin gone, Rex?

REX. Upstairs. Use the gentleman's gentleman.

HESTER. Can I get you a drink?

Confused, REX *improvises, taking a spare glass.*

REX. I've already got one.

HESTER. I expect you'd like some flowers then? To take home to Babs?

She goes to the garden.

REX. But I understand congratulations are in order. You and young Colin here?

ISABEL. That's not settled.

LIONEL. We were discussing it when you came in. I was about to tell her Brother Edwin and I are forming a company to produce a number of plays with pre-London tours and a West End run.

REX. Whatever next?

LIONEL. Yes, and we hope to persuade Isabel to be our leading lady.

Pause while they take this in.

ISABEL. The terms would have to be just right. Would have to specify my roles. Colin's writing a marvellous part for me in which I'm never off the stage. Aren't you, darling?

COLIN. Absolutely. To really stretch you.

The older men laugh as, with thunder and lightning, HESTER *comes back wearing gardening gloves, carrying cut flowers and a bottle of weed-killer.*

HESTER. There! Hybrid Tea Ena Harkness. I know Babs loves them. Now I'm going to mix a fruit-cup for us all. You'd like one, wouldn't you, Rex?

REX. No fear, Hester. I know your cocktails. Positively lethal. Anyway you won't be wanting this weed-killer for that, will you?

He relieves her of it.

HESTER. Oh. I meant to do the crazy paving. Must have got side-tracked.

REX. Easily done. My mind's like a sieve these days. Unless I write everything down, as Colin's doing now.

COLIN. Just another idea for a play.

REX (*taking* COLIN'*s pad and reading*). Middle-aged genteel housewife becomes mass-murderer. That interest you, Isabel?

ISABEL. Middle-aged?

LIONEL. That must be the character part. Eh, boy?

COLIN. Obviously. You're the lead.

ISABEL. Has it got a breakdown in the last act? You know, a long hysterical speech that ends in tears?

REX. That a problem, son?

COLIN (*to her*). You want your pound of flesh, don't you? Well, let's see.

Returns to his writing. Phone rings, stops. Door-chimes.

HESTER. Who can that be? At this hour?

EDWIN (*off*). I'll go.

HESTER. Well, if we're having more company I need another.

She walks into the study, through the wall. They decide to ignore it. The piano plays 'My Hero' and REX, *being nearest, sits and mimes.* ISABEL *sings and the other men join in.* HESTER *hears and looks across, shakes her head and pours more drinks. A parlourmaid in mob-cap, apron, black stockings, etc., enters the living-room. It takes a few moments to see she's* EDWIN. *The piano stops and their singing dies.*

EDWIN. No one there, sir. Just kids ringing and running away, I expect. Boys will be boys, I always say.

LIONEL. Ah, thank you, Gladys.

ISABEL. Hullo again. I was wondering when you were going to put in an appearance.

EDWIN. Yes, ma'am.

REX. Look, missie, why don't you take this bottle and hide it away? Your mistress brought it in by mistake.

EDWIN. She'd lose her head if it wasn't screwed on, sir.

ISABEL. As long as she doesn't pour any on the Mulberry roots, eh, Inspector?

COLIN. What *is* all this about the Mulberry?

EDWIN. I think the young missie means it would be a shame to spoil such luscious fruit.

REX. Never mind that, son. Just get on with that scene for Miss Angel. And, as for you, my dear, I'd advise you not to push your luck, if you take my meaning? If these gents make every effort to accommodate you, you'd best be a good girl, behave yourself, learn to show a little respect to –

ISABEL. To my betters, were you going to say? Meaning those who've never had to fight ... never had to use their nails and teeth, to climb out of the gutter, eh? Always had it easy? Don't try to deny it. You're all against me, with your money and your big house and your pals in the police. Law and order! Don't make me laugh. Jesus, what a world, eh? Fat chance I've got to lead a decent life, making something of myself, when the whole of Society's rotten to the core ...

She throws herself on to the sofa, sobbing hysterically. The rest applaud.

COLIN. Or something on those lines.

REX. I'd say you're on to a winner there, Lionel.

LIONEL. Nothing an audience enjoys more than a woman having hysterics.

ISABEL (*dry-eyed at once*). This isn't yet a leading part. She should have far more to do.

LIONEL. If you say so, my dear.

COLIN. But with you giving her flesh ...

ISABEL. And what about Act Two? What happens? Do the skeletons start rattling in their cupboards? How does Bernie come back? You won't find it easy to cast him if he has to spend the second half waiting for his call. He'd be seriously under-parted.

LIONEL. That's Colin's problem, not ours.

REX. I'm sure the family will do all they can to meet Miss Angel's terms.

COLIN. So – everything's turned out very nicely.

LIONEL. You think so?

COLIN. If I were writing it, I'd call it a happy ending. The hero gets the girl. The villain's sent packing. The future's rosy and not a lot different from the past. The cats have been briefly glimpsed but are now back in the bag. It's all been rounded off in a decently well-made way.

HESTER *comes through the wall with drinks.*

HESTER. Drinkies!

EDWIN. Let me help you, madam.

HESTER. Gladys! You're back.

EDWIN. Oh, I'll never desert you, madam. Unless, that is, you keep rabbiting on about the Mulberry Tree.

Drinks given out, they all gather at the piano and wait during a long pause. They look at HESTER.

HESTER. So. What now?

COLIN (*prompting her*). A toast?

HESTER. Oh, yes, a nice toast. And Gladys must join us. She's almost one of the family.

EDWIN. Oh, madam.

ISABEL. And just to be on the safe side ...

She swaps her glass for LIONEL*'s. They all laugh.*

EDWIN. To the happy couple!

HESTER. Happy families!

COLIN. Success to Boswell Plays!

LIONEL (*touches* ISABEL*'s belly*). And all their forthcoming productions.

ALL. Cheers!

They drink. LIONEL *clutches his throat and staggers. All stare.*

REX. Hello, hello, hello ...

EDWIN. Hester – no! It had all been sorted out.

LIONEL (*sitting up, laughing*). My little joke.

They laugh again. The piano plays 'Nice People' and they glare at the sound-booth.

ACT TWO

A GAME OF SOLDIERS

A spacious and elegant room, furnished with official sofas, armchairs, a desk, coffee-table, etc. On shelves heavy reference books. On a side-table a typewriter. A fender and irons indicate a fireplace in the fourth wall. A portrait of the Queen hangs on the upstage wall. A chandelier above.

Three mahogany doors: A in the stage right wall to an outer office and the building's main entrance; B stage left wall, to other offices and a back way out; C upstage wall, to a walk-in W.C. and cupboard beside two long sash windows that give on to the inner courtyard of St James's Palace, so that we see some of the ancient brick buildings on the far side of a courtyard. Mid-morning daylight.

Music: 'Anything Goes'.

'In olden days a glimpse of stocking
Was looked on as something shocking
But now Lord knows
Anything Goes.'

Plays while DENIS, *a guardsman in bearskin hat and scarlet tunic, bearing his rifle at the slope, marches past one window, on sentry go outside. Passing the next, he peers in at the empty room and moves on out of sight.*

Meanwhile music gives way to radio news.

RADIO NEWSREADER. 1967 is a year which has already seen the legalisation of homosexual acts between adult men. Yesterday the abortion bill cleared its third reading in the Commons.

The sound of a lavatory flush and door C is opened and BILL TRIMMER, *a discreet ex-wing commander, enters, comes down to the main desk, spreads files and documents, checks the lay-out of cigarette-case, ashtray, pencils, etc., on the coffee-table.*

The pop-stars, the Rolling Stones, were cleared of drugs charges today and walked free. In the worst financial crisis for twenty years and following the devaluation of the pound, Mr Callaghan is expected to resign as Chancellor. But Mr Wilson, the Prime Minister, claimed that now the way is clear for economic expansion and a sound future for . . . '

The guardsman returns, sees TRIMMER, *looks left and right and taps on the pane. He gestures him to raise the window and he does, first locking door A.* DENIS *clambers into the room. The news broadcast fades.*

TRIMMER. Are you mad? Your sergeant could easily have seen.

DENIS. I know, but this won't wait. Dead urgent.

TRIMMER. Well, give us a kiss first. Away from the window.

DENIS *moves down and leans his rifle against the desk. His manner is butch, his accent Cockney. They kiss.*

Now, my dear, whatever's the matter? You didn't forget to take your envelope from the mantelpiece?

DENIS. No, darling. No problem there.

TRIMMER. So it can't be money.

Reads DENIS*'s expression.*

Yes, it can.

DENIS. I'm over a barrel. My bird's got me by the short hairs. She's only gone and cheated the starter.

TRIMMER. She's what?

DENIS. She's in the club, up the pole, got one coming.

TRIMMER. Darling, how many times have I told you not to mess with women? Living up to your name, eh?

DENIS. What, Denis?

TRIMMER. Meddler.

DENIS. You can talk. What about Rosemary?

TRIMMER. Rosemary's not a woman, she's my wife. So don't drag her into this. As long as you and I can meet when I'm in town and she's in Haslemere,/ she need never –

DENIS. Look, I can't hang about nattering.

TRIMMER. D'you think I can? With two applicants due any minute?

DENIS. Fact is, sweetie, you've got to help. Getting rid of the kid's going to cost us.

TRIMMER. I can't be held responsible for what you get up to with every old slag/ you pick up round Soho –

DENIS. She's no old slag. She's as respectable as you.

TRIMMER. She sounds it.

DENIS. Does the name Freebody ring a bell?

TRIMMER. That professional virgin?

DENIS. And though I don't fancy being a grass, I can't promise to keep stumm about our relations/ if I'm to be out of pocket –

TRIMMER. All right! How much d'you need and when?

DENIS. A century altogether but half a yard today.

TRIMMER. What's that in English money?

DENIS. Fifty quid. Now. Cash.

TRIMMER. I've only got a tenner on me.

DENIS. Your bank's just up St James's Street.

TRIMMER. But I've got to be here when these chaps arrive. Won't lunch-time do?

DENIS. No. She wants cash in the bank before she books the clinic.

PARROTT (*outside door A*). Bill! Are you in there?

They freeze.

TRIMMER (*calls*). Coming! Hang on!

DENIS *tries the window but can't move it.*

Get out for Chrissake!

DENIS. It's stuck.

TRIMMER *tries too. No luck.*

PARROTT (*off*). Just want to use the phone.

TRIMMER (*to* DENIS). Get in here!

Opens C. We see the lavatory with a chain cistern, surrounded by shelves of manuscripts and files from floor to ceiling. TRIMMER *hustles* DENIS *in.*

(*Calls.*) I'm getting into my trousers, sir. (*To* DENIS.) Pull the flush!

DENIS *does.* TRIMMER *shuts the door, moves across to door A but* DENIS *comes from C and whistles to him to show he's left his rifle.* TRIMMER *jiggles key in lock as* DENIS *runs to retrieve it.*

Sorry, sir, this key's on the blink.

As DENIS *regains C and shuts it,* TRIMMER *lets in* PARROTT, *an ex-Guards officer, politic and reassuring, carrying papers.*

PARROTT. Morning, Bill, if I might just use this room for a private call before these applicants arrive ... Would you mind?

TRIMMER. Lord, no. I'm about to pop out to the florist.

PARROTT. Something to celebrate?

TRIMMER. Rosemary's Baby.

PARROTT. Really? At fifty? Is that wise?

TRIMMER. Birthday! Not baby, no. I was thinking of that film.

PARROTT. Fine. Glad to hear it. I'll hold the fort. Wish her many happy/ returns from me –

TRIMMER. Thank you.

PARROTT. And don't be long. Don't want to be left with these two applicants ...

TRIMMER *goes by B.* PARROTT *at once dials a number, while* DENIS *begins to escape from C.*

Meddler?

DENIS *springs to attention.*

Jack Meddler?

At this name DENIS stares at PARROTT. *As he part-turns upstage,* DENIS *holds his position and* PARROTT *doesn't notice.*

Parrott here. Remember I told you the phone in my own office may be tapped? ... Special Branch, I dare say. Obviously I can't have it known I'm talking to the press so I'm using another extension.

TRIMMER *arrives outside the stuck window, tries it without success, crosses to the other.* DENIS, *seeing him, moves crabwise across behind* PARROTT.

I promised you a scoop and now's the moment ... Not directly about the Prime Minister no, though it all goes to confirm what we already suspected ... not only that he's a Soviet agent ... oh, yes, since long before he took office ... before he even became Labour Party Leader ...

TRIMMER *tries the second window, then sees that* DENIS *is loose in the room. As* DENIS *arrives at window 2, door A is opened, hiding him, and* PRUE FREEBODY, *an officious – but somehow provocative – secretary enters.*

PRUE. I'm sorry, Colonel, I thought you'd want to know the supplicants are here.

PARROTT. Supplicants?

PRUE. Applicants.

PARROTT. We mustn't think of them like that.

PRUE. No.

PARROTT. Still. Won't hurt them to cool their heels a bit.

PRUE. Absolutely not, sir.

She goes, revealing DENIS. TRIMMER *has no more success with the new window, mimes a great shrug to* DENIS, *signals to him to hide again and goes on trying the window.*

PARROTT (*into the phone*). But, of course, that's common

knowledge since old Gollywog of the KGB spilt the beans to MI6 and the C.I.A. about how Gaitskell was poisoned to clear the way for you-know-who.

DENIS, *moving back to door C is intrigued by* PARROTT'*s speech and stands with C open, listening, till* PARROTT *turns upstage and he quickly goes, closing C.* PARROTT *sees* TRIMMER *at the window.* TRIMMER *waves and goes across the courtyard.*

No, this is something new ... and more far-reaching. Right here in this stagnant backwater, I've uncovered an even more sinister conspiracy ... not on the phone, not now. I'll be through here about one. Meet you in the reading room of the London Library at – say – quarter past. Nice and quiet there. Fine.

Puts down phone, switches on intercom.

Miss Freebody? You can show them in now.

Turns off and goes by B. DENIS *comes from C and follows to B, opens it cautiously as* PRUE *enters at A, sees his back view, gives a little scream and slams A on someone following on. A cry of pain off. She locks the door.*

PRUE. Denis! What on earth are you doing in here?

DENIS. Trying to get out. The window's stuck. I climbed in to put the squeeze on Trimmer.

PRUE. Any luck?

DENIS. A doddle. He's gone to cash a cheque.

PRUE *looks out by door B then shuts it.*

PRUE. Not that way. It's teeming with tea-ladies.

DENIS. If I'm not back on duty pronto, the sarnt-major will have my balls.

PRUE. Well? Everyone else has.

DENIS. Now, now ...

He gives her behind a squeeze as she bends to try the window.

PRUE. Keep your hands to yourself, d'you hear me!

DENIS. Bit late to be coy now, darling. About six weeks too late, didn't you say?

PRUE. A moment's madness. You caught me on the rebound. Perhaps you'd rather I had the child?

DENIS. No bloody fear. Her Indoors would kill me.

She pushes him into C, shuts door but he opens it again.

And as for your boyfriend the colonel, he's a few bricks short of a shithouse. D'you know, he only reckons Harold Wilson's a Russian spy.

PRUE. I'm sure if the colonel believes it –

DENIS. The Prime Minister a Commie? Pull the other, darling. He's not even a leftie.

Knock on A. She shuts C on DENIS *again and moves to open A and admit* RANDY HOGAN *and* NICK JOHNSON. RANDY*'s the same as* BERNIE *but now with more expensive clothes.* NICK*'s like Colin and has a brief-case.* RANDY *holds a handkerchief to his nose.*

PRUE. So sorry to keep you waiting. Oh, a nosebleed?

RANDY (*lying on the sofa*). You slammed the door on it.

PRUE. Sorry.

NICK. And locked it.

RANDY. What is it we mustn't see, eh?

PRUE. Can I ask you not to mention it to Colonel Parrott? He detests anything underhand or two-faced. He says this office can't do the job it has to if there's even a hint of hanky-panky.

RANDY. An officer and a gentleman, is he?

PRUE. Coldstream Guards, retired.

NICK. So what sort of hanky-panky?

PRUE. Only a surprise party.

NICK. For the colonel?

RANDY. Involving a guardsman? I caught a butcher's before the door/ hit me in the face.

PRUE. Ah. Not a real one.

RANDY. No?

PRUE. No. One of the transport pool in fancy dress. Now do make yourselves at home. There will be coffee in the fullness of time. The Assistant Comptroller knows you're here.

She goes by A.

RANDY. Surprise party my arsehole! Bit of the other, if you ask me. (*Going to the desk, scanning the files.*) This is the same list they sent us. Jesus Christ, sod, Billingsgate, bastard, tits and arse ... No surprises there. What's this about Harold Wilson?

NICK. They suspected him of murdering Gaitskell.

RANDY. I thought you were on Wilson's side.

NICK. That seems to have escaped them.

RANDY. Hang about – (*Taking out pages from further down.*) Look at this.

NICK. D'you think we should? If someone came –

RANDY. Reader's report on *Foreign Bodies*, a play in one act by Nick Johnson. Never shown us this, have they?

NICK *goes to look.*

'This struck me as a particularly jejune piece of rubbish in the currently modish manner of menace and absurdity. The plot is made more offensive by taking place in a respectable home. Probably deliberately.'

Door C is opened and DENIS *comes out, cautiously. Intent on reading, they don't see.*

What's jejune mean?

NICK. *Jejeune*? Callow, juvenile ...

RANDY. Fucking sauce! Here, I could do with a slash. Reckon there's a bog round here?

He turns as DENIS *retreats slamming the door. They look at door A.* RANDY *goes to it.*

D'you hear that? Someone slammed the door? I'll stand guard over here while you read it out.

NICK. 'Two intruders threaten to blackmail a young actor's apparently law-abiding family who are later shown to be anything but. The mother poisons the male outsider and the young and innocent girl – who is nothing of the sort – agrees to stay with the family on terms which mean all their secrets will be kept hidden. The plot is presumably contrived to demonstrate that decency is a fraud and everyone – even a high-ranking police officer – is venal, unprincipled and sexually depraved – '

Door B is opened and TRIMMER *looks in.* NICK *quickly hides the file.*

TRIMMER. Ah! There will be coffee, in the fullness of time.

Goes. RANDY *crosses, opens B and looks after him.*

RANDY. Excuse me. D'you know where there's a – ...

Shuts it again.

NICK. 'The characters lack all the qualities one hopes to find in even the most ordinary drama: grace, breadth of vision, power of utterance, at the very least common humanity. Perhaps some sign of an original mind may have justified a licence but the style and plot are a long way after Pinter and Orton, not to mention *Arsenic and Old Lace*, and I can find no good reason to recommend this play and every reason to suppress it.'

Closes file, crosses to coffee-table and takes a cigarette.

My first review.

RANDY. Good job we saw it. Now we know what we're up against.

NICK. Come on, this is hopeless. I knew it would be. Let's go.

RANDY. Bollocks. We knew we'd have to do some horse-trading ... give 'em a sod-off here for a jig-jig there.

He moves about the room while NICK *sits miserably smoking.*

Now ... having been in the schmatter trade I know dealing. I know the way these geezers run the world. They're top drawer,

I'm bargain basement, we understand each other. And you're pig in the middle. Or more precisely the lower middle. So be a good boy and leave it to me –

NICK. And if I disagree with what you say?

RANDY. That's how they'll play it. Try to split the opposition. Divide and rule.

He tries door C but it's locked.

NICK. You saying I'm not to speak?

RANDY. All I mean is: you're the author, this play's your baby, you'll be like a fucking whatdyoucallit, a tigress with her cub, right? You'll over-react.

NICK. I know we need this licence but if you think I'm going to let them cut the play to shreds after all the work you and I have done –

TRIMMER *appears outside the window, urgently looking for* DENIS. RANDY *faces upstage, watching him.*

RANDY. What's this dickhead up to?

NICK. He's the one who looked in at the door.

RANDY *opens window 1 with ease.* TRIMMER *stares.*

RANDY. Need any help, mate?

TRIMMER *waves 'no' and moves off left.* RANDY *shuts the window.*

Court jester, d'you reckon? After all, this *is* a fucking palace. (*Turns back into the room.*) No, give-and-take's the name of the game. Softly-softly. Agree to anything. Later on we'll shove it all back. Another principle of the ruling class: nothing is forever.

NICK. Except the ruling class.

RANDY. Them least of all. They're for the chop.

Outside TRIMMER *returns, still looking, goes off, right.*

NICK. How can you believe that, faced with St James's? The gentlemen's clubs, the handmade boot and cigar shops, the grace-and-favour houses, her lot round the corner –

Points to the Queen's picture.

RANDY. Rip-e for the picking. It's our turn to have all that.

NICK. Would you want it though?

RANDY. Don't you?

NICK. I'd rather destroy it.

PRUE *opens A and looks in.*

PRUE. Ah. Not here yet?

And goes.

RANDY. You mean – if you can't have it, why should they? Churchill called that the politics of envy.

NICK. Pretty good from someone born in Blenheim Palace.

RANDY. Never fear. In twenty years this'll be ours. She and her lot will be on superannuation.

NICK. Randy, I'm only too aware the play would never have got this far without you. It's you that persuaded the theatre governors to produce a one-act play by an unknown writer. You know how grateful/ I am for –

RANDY. Bullshit! I'm the one who's grateful. For the chance to work in the theatre after all that cobblers on telly. First time for years. Which is why I'm determined we get this licence. Only be prepared to swallow more humble pie than you think you can stomach.

PARROTT *enters B.* TRIMMER *follows, closing door.*

PARROTT. Good morning. So sorry to keep you.

TRIMMER. This is Colonel Parrott, the Lord Chamberlain's Assistant Controller. And I'm the Assistant's assistant. Wing Commander Bill Trimmer.

RANDY. Randy Hogan.

PARROTT. The producer?

RANDY. Director. The producer puts up the money.

PARROTT. Absolutely. So you're Mr Boswell?

NICK. Johnson. Nick Johnson.

PARROTT. Boswell's Johnson. You see my thinking? I'm much obliged to you. And for sparing your valuable time for an exchange of views. We know how busy you must be. Sit-ye-down, please.

TRIMMER *leads them to the sofa and chairs.* PARROTT *presses a buzzer on the intercom.*

There should be coffee in the fullness of time.

TRIMMER. Either of you care for a Nelson?

Offers the cigarette-case. NICK *stubs out the last, takes a new one.* PRUE *comes in at A with a pad and pencil.*

PARROTT. You've met Miss Freebody? Or perhaps, in keeping with the new informal spirit of Swinging London, we may call you Prudence?

PRUE. Prudence is what I'm generally known as. Or have been till now.

She lets out an unexpected sob and reaches for a handkerchief.

I do beg your pardon.

He rises and solicitously places a chair for her downstage, facing up. She simpers gratefully and sits to take notes. TRIMMER *is at the window looking out for* DENIS. PARROTT *sees.*

PARROTT. Are we expecting anyone else, Bill?

TRIMMER. No, sir. But the palace buildings are a never-ending source of pleasure to my eye.

PARROTT. Oh, most agreeable. (*Then to* NICK *and* RANDY.) As you know, the gateway is in fact the only survival from Henry the Eighth's Tudor palace which was in turn built upon the site of a mediaeval leper hospital. Many people nowadays consider that a very suitable place to house the official censor.

They all laugh.

Though, as you may know, we do not think of ourselves as

censors but li-censors. We are here not to prohibit but to allow. All things being equal.

RANDY. Equal to what?

PARROTT. I'm sorry?

RANDY. All things being equal to what?

TRIMMER. The colonel means that since 1737 when the task fell to the Chamberlain most plays have been allowed without a quibble.

PARROTT. As you know.

RANDY. No, I didn't.

NICK *looks uneasily at* RANDY.

PARROTT. Though it's not a task he much enjoys –

TRIMMER. Which may well be why he passes it to us.

PARROTT. Indeed many of us here rather concur with those of your colleagues who advocate abolishing this particular power altogether –

TRIMMER. A consummation devoutly to be wished.

PARROTT. – so that we may get on with managing the Royal household.

RANDY. Being Master of the Queen's Toilet Rolls?

PARROTT. As you so wittily say. Awarding warrants to butchers, bakers and candlestick-makers –

TRIMMER. Upping the royal swans –

RANDY. Oops! Sounds as though it should be on the list.

PARROTT. As I think Bill meant to imply. However, until that happy day we're duty bound to protect the public from gratuitous unpleasantness. Which brings us to your play –

Opens file. TRIMMER *too.* NICK *supplies* RANDY *with a copy from his brief-case.*

– which I fear we find upsetting on a number of counts.

RANDY. It's meant to be.

PARROTT. I'm sorry?

RANDY. Upsetting.

PARROTT. And our job is to see that it's not.

He smiles agreeably. NICK *glares at* RANDY.

As you know.

NICK. And – honestly – we're very keen to help all we can. That's why we're here.

RANDY *stands angrily.*

RANDY. First off, I could do with a slash. Where's the nearest bog?

PARROTT. The door beside the windows.

RANDY. I already tried. It's locked.

PARROTT. Locked?

He moves upstage to try the door. PRUE *stands.*

PRUE. Yes, sir. From last night. And the key's gone missing.

TRIMMER. Can't be. I had it open just this –

He looks at PRUE, *she looks at him. The penny drops. He stops.*

Come to think of it, that *was* last night.

PARROTT. But, Bill, weren't you in there when I tried to get in just now?

TRIMMER. Don't see how I can have been if it's been locked since last night. And if Miss Freebody – (*Relishing the name.*) says so,/ then I think we must –

PARROTT. In which case, the nearest is along this corridor here, Mr Morgan –

RANDY. Hogan.

He leads RANDY *to B, opens it and gives directions.*

PARROTT. – past the fire extinguishers on your left and take the stairs beside the phone-box, down one flight and keep bearing left till you come to another hall before a storage room.

RANDY *goes,* PARROTT *shuts the door and returns.*

Exhausting hike. That's why I had this one put in. It shares a space with some old scripts we didn't pass. We thought it the best place for them, eh, Bill?

TRIMMER. And, of course, if we ever *lost* the mastery of the toilet rolls –

PARROTT. Quite.

He mimes tearing up a script. They laugh.

Though perhaps we shouldn't be saying that with an author in our midst. Only jesting, Mr Boswell.

NICK. Johnson.

PARROTT. As you say. Now may I ask – you've only given us the first act. When can we expect the other?

NICK. No. That's it. All there is.

PARROTT. But, as you know, that won't make an evening.

NICK. Randy hasn't fixed yet on the second half. Could be an early Coward or Rattigan.

PARROTT. Ah, yes, that'll cheer everyone up. *And* there'll be an interval. Often the best part of the evening. Bill, did you too feel the play needs a second act?

TRIMMER. You and I are bound to because, you see, we're old enough to have grown up with well-made plays that had a beginning, a middle and an end.

PARROTT. Quite so. This one, with the greatest possible respect, seems to have a beginning and the beginning of a middle but no sign of an end.

NICK. Where I feel, if anything, it's almost too well-made, everything accounted for,/ the ends tied up –

PARROTT. Well, never mind. Not our job to tell you what to say, only what you can't. You have the list of our disallowances? Which is the first, Bill?

TRIMMER. Page six, sir. 'Jesus Christ!' and on eleven 'God Almighty'.

NICK. You mean Christ, God and Almighty are dirty words?

PARROTT. Dirty, no. Blasphemous, very much so. When used as oaths.

TRIMMER. Which would infringe item (d) of the 1909 Joint Select Committee recommendations 'That nothing should do violence to the sentiment of religious reverence'.

Takes a tome from the shelf and shows him.

NICK. 1909?

TRIMMER. Our Bible. You can't insult the deity, actual persons, living or lately dead, or the heads of friendly foreign powers.

PARROTT. Which would at the moment include many countries we may not morally approve of. States, for example, where citizens don't enjoy privileges that are the inborn right of every Briton. Where, for starters, there's no such animal as Free Speech. And any attempt at it is stifled by a junta of ageing military men. So – I wonder if any aesthetic injury would result from our young hero – if that is what he is – saying 'Bless my soul!' instead?

NICK. 'Soul's all right, is it?

PARROTT. Bill? Where do we stand on 'soul'?

TRIMMER. Very much depends on the context. For example 'mother' would cause no offence per se but 'motherfucker' would.

NICK. Though 'Oedipus Rex' would be all right?

PARROTT. Ah, motherfucker, yes. Good case in point. I'm obliged to you. Grade A product. Greek tragedy automatically gets a licence.

TRIMMER. Also covered by the exemption granted all plays preceding the first Licensing Act of 1737. Though even there we may have to look at the business.

PARROTT. Ah, yes. So incest in dialogue okay but no gratuitous insertion of hanky-panky with Mama.

He, TRIMMER *and* PRUE *laugh.* NICK *doesn't.*

You can laugh. You'd be surprised what they try to smuggle through. We have to be as eagle-eyed as customs men here. As sensitive to a whiff of filth as the nose of a truffle-pig.

NICK. But don't you agree that in the late sixties calls on Christ or Jesus are pretty common?

TRIMMER. They are indeed. Common as muck.

NICK. I mean common*place*.

PARROTT. All the more reason for us to discourage them. Good try, Mr Boswell –

TRIMMER, NICK *and* PRUE. Johnson! –

PARROTT. – but no. Can we agree on some other familiar oath? 'Hell's bells'? 'Blow me down'? (*And as* NICK *shakes his head, amazed.*) It's got the same meaning.

NICK. But not the same force.

TRIMMER. We have a dictionary of slang here. And *Roget's Thesaurus*. Miss Freebody?

Again he gloats on the name. She glares at him. PRUE *fetches several of the books as* RANDY *returns by B.*

RANDY. Quite a tour of the palace. I think I passed the leper hospital.

PARROTT. It's too much, Prue. We can't go traipsing far and wide every time we want a pee. See if you can trace the key.

PRUE. Yessir.

RANDY *rejoins the huddle. Unseen by any but* TRIMMER, *she unlocks* C *and signals to* DENIS *to come out.*

NICK. Colonel Parrott's suggested 'Stone the crows' for 'Christ Almighty'.

PARROTT. No, no. 'Blow me down'.

RANDY. Seriously?

NICK. It's growing on me.

RANDY. Might have been a bit near the bone in 1850 but now?!

DENIS *cautiously emerges from* C. PRUE *leads him towards*

B, trying to conceal him but his bearskin shows above her head.

NICK. Right. It's exactly the sort of outdated thing Colin might have to say when he's staying with his old-fashioned parents. It helps demonstrate the mealy-mouthed world which Bernie will later invade with his street values.

PARROTT. Always glad to be of help.

TRIMMER *has moved up to* DENIS *and* PRUE *and now offers him a wad of money, which* DENIS *takes and passes to* PRUE. TRIMMER *then helps shield* DENIS *on the way to B.*

RANDY. You agree to everything you'll end up with nothing.

NICK. We want to get the play licensed, don't we? And this happens to be a truthful observation.

PARROTT. Please! You must find alternatives you approve. The bookmark's for the section on general exclamations of wonder. Though there is –

Seeing TRIMMER*'s missing from the group.*

Where's Bill got to now?

TRIMMER *and* PRUE, *shielding* DENIS, *freeze halfway to B as* PARROTT *turns.* TRIMMER *jumps to attention.*

TRIMMER. Sir?

PARROTT. Where's that list of absolutely verboten words we drew up for guidance?

TRIMMER. In the desk drawer?

PARROTT. Right. Let's see ...

He opens drawers as TRIMMER *and* PRUE *sidle on towards B.*

And, Prue, why aren't you looking for that key?

PRUE. I'm just going, sir.

They reach B as it is opened and a tea-trolley is pushed in. A burst of banter offstage. Quickly PRUE, TRIMMER *and* DENIS *shuffle back towards C, push* DENIS *in again and shut it.* DAPHNE, *a middle-aged woman in overalls, follows the trolley.* NICK *and* RANDY *are reading the dictionaries.* PARROTT *returns to his desk to look for the list.*

DAPHNE. . . . so if he tries that again with me, I shall turn round and tell him where to put it . . .

NICK. 'Oh hey day, halloo, indeed, really, humph, good gracious, by jove, by George, by Jingo, well only think, lack-a-daisy, hoity-toity, . . . '

DAPHNE. Morning, gentlemen, turning brighter!

PARROTT. Ah, good morning, Daphne. D'you think it'll hold for the weekend?

DAPHNE. We shall have to keep our fingers crossed. And our legs, as my hubbie always says.

She sets out cups and saucers on the trolley.

PARROTT. I fear your husband's a scandalous example to those of us who are trying to keep the party clean.

He sees PRUE *and* TRIMMER.

Found it, Prue?

TRIMMER (*pretending to shake* C). It's still locked.

PRUE. Just going, Sah.

PRUE *exits A.*

DAPHNE. He means no harm. It's just his way. He hardly knows he's doing it half the time. Never had the advantage of an education.

TRIMMER *has rejoined the men downstage.*

RANDY. 'Fuck a duck, fuck this for a lark – for a pantomime – for a game of soldiers – '

TRIMMER. Out of the question. One of the shortlist of proscribed words that will never be spoken on the stage as long as this office survives.

RANDY. Though they're spoken every day in the street.

TRIMMER. Not in St James's Street. Not in our street in Haslemere.

Unseen by anyone, C *is slowly opened and* DENIS *emerges with his rifle. He creeps to the window* RANDY *opened (1) and easily opens it, climbs into courtyard, comes to attention and marches off.*

DAPHNE. Coffee all round, gents? Anyone apart from Colonel Parrott prefer tea?

PARROTT. Bless you, Daphne, for remembering. What should we do without you?

DAPHNE. You'll be finding out next year when I retire.

PARROTT. 'Change and decay in all around I see ... '

DAPHNE. You'll soon get used to young Tracy, I've trained her what to expect. She knows the way you like it. Hot and strong. No milk and a slice of lemon.

NICK. Black for me, please.

RANDY. White. Three sugars. Thanks, love.

DAPHNE. You're like me, sir, a sweet tooth. I just can't leave it alone. I say to my husband, 'Go on then, just one more. Put it in.'

RANDY. You only live once.

DAPHNE. 'Course, he likes to see me enjoy it. He stirs it that well ... swings his spoon round and round – ding-dong – it seems like hours –

PRUE *returns by A.*

PRUE. No luck, I'm afraid.

DAPHNE. – till I wonder if he's ever going to take it out and shake it.

PRUE. But they're all searching.

PARROTT. Prue, I'm blessed if I can find that list now.

PRUE *stands close to him, leans over, opens the centre drawer between his legs.*

PRUE. Excuse me, if I may just reach down here – yes, there it is, sir.

PARROTT. So it is. Take it out, there's a good girl –

Everyone watches as she reaches for the list, reels slightly. Unsteadily she makes for her chair downstage and sits.

And read it aloud.

PRUE. Fuck, shit, tits, turd, fart, prick, cunt, bollocks, buggery –

PARROTT. The feeling here being that there are always alternative and acceptable words if authors put their minds to it. Give an example, Prue.

PRUE. Cunt, sir? Plum-tree, pudendum, basket, scabbard, vagina, mons veneris, Shooter's Hill –

NICK. But as a term of abuse? 'Fornicate elsewhere, you mons veneris!'

PARROTT. Not our problem, I fear. Our job is to spot it when you try to slip it in.

RANDY. Slip it in? That's acceptable, is it?

They all laugh but RANDY, *who scowls.*

PARROTT. Come on, gentlemen, we've a lot to get through. What have you agreed to instead of 'Christ Almighty'?

NICK. I quite like 'Holy Moses'. The sort of thing no Englishman has said for fifty years –

PARROTT. Bill? Moses? Permissible, I think?

TRIMMER. Oh, quite. Old Testament passes for –

He makes a gesture, finger on nose.

NICK. What?

TRIMMER. You know – Hebrew.

PARROTT. Long as it's not C of E.

NICK. OK, Randy?

RANDY. Your play. You want to let them chop off your bollocks – or is it testicles? –

PARROTT. Prue?

PRUE. Cullions, scrotum, cobbler's awls, orchestra stalls –

TRIMMER. Our resident expert.

DAPHNE. I've served coffee over here, case some gets spilt on the colonel's leather top.

TRIMMER (*spying them on the trolley*). Marie biscuits, Boudoirs ... Daphne, I do believe you've procured us custard creams.

DAPHNE. Don't breathe a word to next door, mind.

TRIMMER. My lips are sealed.

PARROTT. Page eleven we have the first of a number of references to paederasty.

DAPHNE. They're always on at me ... 'How is it *we* never get custard creams?'

PARROTT. 'Sod, no-balls Boswell, ponce, a reference to chorus boys and the father in a maid's uniform.'

DAPHNE. They say, 'Why is it always Marie biscuits?'

PARROTT. In this office, homosexuality has had a rather chequered career. Yes, Bill? You're the authority.

TRIMMER (*alarmed*). Authority, me? What can you mean, Colonel?

PARROTT. On its history. Apropos this office.

TRIMMER. Ah, quite.

DAPHNE. They say, 'We never even get Garibaldis.'

PARROTT. I say, Daphne, there aren't enough custard creams to go round.

DAPHNE. I counted them out. Four.

PARROTT. But there are five of us. Unless you want Miss Freebody to make do with a ginger nut.

PRUE. I'm quite happy with a Boudoir, really.

TRIMMER (*laughs at the double-meaning*). Yers ...

PARROTT. Out of the question. Can you work your irresistible magic again, Daphne? I'm much obliged. Where were we?

DAPHNE. Custard creams don't grow on trees, you know ...

She goes off resentfully by B.

PARROTT. Bloody good job that old cow's going. Where'd we got to, Prue?

PRUE. Homosexuality, Colonel.

PARROTT. Bill?

TRIMMER. Until 1958 it was totally banned from the English stage. Now it's permissible provided One: it's seen as a pitiable affliction and Two: no erotic arousal takes place between males.

RANDY. Though it's now legal between consenting adults?

TRIMMER (*suddenly furious*). Going to the lavatory's legal but you'd hardly want to see it on the stage.

RANDY. What's the ruling on nellies? Bull dykes? Collars-and-ties?

TRIMMER. If you mean lesbians, it's allowed in principle, as it was thought a total ban might arouse the curiosity of adolescent gals. Most females don't know it exists till they read about it.

PARROTT. And hasn't *their* misery to be brought out too?

TRIMMER. Oh, yes. Even more so.

RANDY. OK being bent as long as you don't enjoy it?

PRUE. If I may, sir? The issue here isn't homosexuality per se but the terminology.

PARROTT. Thank you, Prue. Most grateful. I hope there's no danger of *your* leaving us.

PRUE. None whatsoever, sir.

TRIMMER. Not now anyway.

PARROTT. Sorry?

TRIMMER. Nothing.

PARROTT. Thank the Lord for that!

He smiles. She simpers. TRIMMER *scowls.*

RANDY (*consulting the slang dictionary*). Queer, arse bandit, buttfucker, fag, fairy, fruit, gay, ginger, iron hoof – and I reckon a blue-movie maker from Soho would have all that on the tip of his tongue.

PARROTT. Ah, yes, Bernie the director. A uniquely charmless character.

RANDY (*reading on*). . . . nance, nelly, one of those, shirt-lifter, windjammer –

PARROTT. We're in a semantic glory-hole with this one.

NICK (*finding it*). Queer. *Roget* has it under Ridiculousness. Rum, quizzical, waggish, monstrosity –

PARROTT. Look here, I don't think anyone in the permissive society of Swinging London is going to object to 'pansies'. What d'you say, Bill?

NICK. 'Nancy-boys'?

PRUE. There is a precedent for both, sir.

PARROTT. Nancy-boys. Agreed, Mr Boswell? Jolly good.

They all make notes.

Now – erotic gestures –

RANDY. I wouldn't let them do it to my play.

PARROTT. But you may not be quite as keen to see this play on the stage as Mr Boswell is.

NICK.
TRIMMER.
PRUE. } Johnson.

RANDY. But he won't, will he? Only the mutilated remains.

NICK. We haven't done much damage yet.

PARROTT. What's our position on erotic gestures?

TRIMMER. All disallowed. And a licence would have a proviso proscribing sexual display . . . the girl touching the old uncle between his legs. Or implying that the old may seduce the young. No funny business with the mother and the young girl.

NICK. It's wrong because they're old?

PARROTT. The old may not be depicted as voyeurs.

TRIMMER. So that when Bernie physically assaults Isabel, their elders may not watch.

NICK. So what to do?

TRIMMER. Could the old people be got offstage before any funny business starts?

PARROTT. And then got back on afterwards'.

NICK. They'll have seen it at rehearsal.

TRIMMER. But they won't be *seen* to have seen it.

PARROTT. What the eye doesn't see . . .

RANDY. Christ!

RANDY *moves upstage, his mind blown. As he reaches the window,* DENIS *marches into view and stands performing rifle drill, facing upstage.* TRIMMER, *seeing, chokes on his tea.*

TRIMMER. Sorry.

NICK. I'm still amazed you can censor the business.

PARROTT. Lord, yes. For example here where the father says 'Not one of your stiff ones'. Is that accompanied by a gesture?

NICK. Sorry?

PARROTT. A gesture – like so – ?

PARROTT *stands and makes a downward movement with one hand.* RANDY *comes to see.* TRIMMER *has sneaked upstage to look from the window at* DENIS, *who turns into profile. They converse by signs.* PRUE*'s facing down.* RANDY *and* NICK *still bewildered.*

RANDY. I'm not with you, no.

PARROTT. Miss Freebody – could you help me? Imagine you're the mother and I'm the father Mr Boswell.

RANDY }
PRUE } Johnson ...

NICK. No, Boswell. The colonel's got it right.

PARROTT. If at first you don't succeed.

PRUE *joins* PARROTT *and repeats his gesture near his crotch.*

Like so –

DAPHNE *returns with one biscuit in her hand, throws it at* PRUE.

DAPHNE. One custard cream. Now. Any more for any more?

She starts refilling cups as DENIS *sees her and marches off.*

NICK. No, you've lost us, I'm afraid.

PARROTT. Bill –

He turns to find TRIMMER *at the window. He at once comes down.*

You're a far better actor than I am –

TRIMMER. Had to be in the prison camp. Mostly in drag.

PARROTT. Drag?

TRIMMER. Frocks.

PARROTT. Quite. So could you possibly demonstrate? 'Not one of your stiff ones!'

TRIMMER *repeats the gesture and knocks a cup from* DAPHNE*'s hand, spilling tea over* PARROTT, *who starts moaning.*

DAPHNE. Oh, my Gawd!

PRUE. Really! How clumsy can you get! You've scalded the colonel.

PRUE *mops him with her tiny handkerchief.*

DAPHNE. How did I know the Wing Commander was going to flap his hand about like that?

TRIMMER (*bridling*). Flap his hand?! Exactly what/ are you implying?

PRUE. We've been discussing it the last five minutes.

DAPHNE. And what are you suggesting? I never listen to a word you gentlemen say. What's she suggesting, sir? Don't you get suggestive with me, missy!

PARROTT. Never mind that. Mop me up. I'm soaked with hot tea.

DAPHNE *moves up to* C.

PRUE. Where are you going?

DAPHNE. There's a cloth in the toilet. And running water.

PRUE. No, there isn't.

DAPHNE *reaches and starts to open the door.* PRUE *slams it shut and stands across it, arms outstretched.*

DAPHNE. What d'you mean, there isn't? It's in the tap.

PRUE. It's locked.

DAPHNE. The tap?

PRUE. The W.C. We've lost the key.

DAPHNE. I've just had it open!

PRUE. Impossible!

TRIMMER *pushes by and opens it.* PRUE*'s alarmed and turns to hide from the discovery only to see* DENIS *marching back outside. He waves and exits.* DAPHNE *goes into* C *as* TRIMMER *and* PRUE *mime question and answer.*
Downstage PARROTT *has taken off his trousers.*

PARROTT. Don't bother with that, Daphne. Take these to be pressed.

PRUE (*also grasping the trousers*). I'll do it, sir.

DAPHNE. Oh no you won't. What do you know about the world below stairs, eh? A place of steaming trousers and singing kettles, puddings simmering in double boilers, a world of spotted dicks to remind all these gentlemen of their school-days?

PRUE. Precious little, I'm glad to say.

She lets the trousers go and DAPHNE *goes off with them by B.*

PARROTT. What's the matter with her?

PRUE. She seems to be in the grip of passion, sir.

PARROTT. At her age?

PRUE. It *is* her age. Her time of life.

PARROTT. Then she must go before next year. This office has to be above reproach.

PRUE. I've made a note, sir. Early retirement.

PARROTT. Jolly good. Now –

PRUE. 'Not one of your stiff ones,' sir.

TRIMMER. We have to be sure she's not envisaging a tumescent penis.

NICK. The tea-lady?

TRIMMER. Hester in the play.

All three repeat the gesture. RANDY *and* NICK *amazed.*

NICK. Oh, no, nothing of that sort. Holy Moses, no! Great Scott! Hell's bells! No, Hester's always fetching or demanding drinks. She serves another gin, that's all.

TRIMMER *and* PARROTT *look at each other.*

PARROTT. Ah ... well ... we evidently got that wrong.

TRIMMER. My fault, sir. *I* introduced the penis.

PARROTT. You'd better withdraw it then. At the double.

The censors and PRUE *laugh.*

I'm afraid that in this office a dirty mind is an occupational hazard.

TRIMMER. Our motto has to be 'When in doubt, take it out'.

RANDY. Is that accompanied by a gesture?

Everyone but RANDY *laughs.*

NICK. I've never really cared for that line anyway. Let's cut it. It could be misconstrued and get the wrong kind of laugh. As we see.

TRIMMER. Some of the stuff that comes in here you'd hardly believe. Anything from the RSC for a start.

PARROTT. The Royal Sodomites Company, eh, Bill?

TRIMMER. The Randy Scopophiliacs Consortium.

PARROTT (*down to the front, shows the tongs*). What d'you think we use these for, in a smokeless zone? I won't touch the stuff.

TRIMMER. With some producers, if it says 'He moves upstage', we have to ask if he's wearing trousers.

PARROTT *moves upstage, not wearing trousers.*

PARROTT. And if it's a woman, if she's wearing clothes at all! It's not that we're prudes, you understand. But people have to be protected. An occasional flash of artistically justified nudity's all very well but where will it end?

RANDY. I know this line. The slippery slope?

PARROTT. Nude Wagner at Covent Garden.

TRIMMER. Nude Communion at Westminster?

NICK. Full-frontal Prime Minister's Question Time?

RANDY. The House of Lords?

TRIMMER. Perish the thought!

They are enjoying this, though PARROTT*'s serious.*

NICK. Trooping the Colour?

PARROTT *recoils, clears throat, gestures at Queen's picture.*

Side-saddle, of course.

PARROTT. Now, now. Let's press on.

PRUE. *Ten Little Niggers*, Colonel.

PARROTT. What's wrong with that?

TRIMMER. Question from one of our examiners whether we shouldn't say 'Ten Little Darkies'. Or 'Ten Little Coloureds'. It was apparently thought it might give offence to members of the Commonwealth.

PARROTT. It gives offence to me to have the Brigade of Guards, the Judiciary and the entire police force represented as a shower of perverts but I have to put up with it or we'd never have any new plays on at all. Now some may consider that a damned good thing but the Lord Chamberlain's office is not the Thought Police. This is a free country. D'you know, in South Africa, they aren't allowed to read *Black Beauty*, the story of a horse? They'll be banning the Black and White Minstrels next.

The others laugh slightly at this and more as he starts to fantasise.

Or the golliwogs on the marmalade. They'll be telling us we can't tell jokes about Irishmen. Or Jews. Or any foreigners at all.

TRIMMER. Or mothers-in-law.

PARROTT. Or wives? Can't make fun of dwarfs? Case we hurt their feelings. Or pensioners.

PRUE. Or Nancy-boys.

TRIMMER. Or pregnant women.

PARROTT. Or tramps or drunks. Cripples, spastics, epileptics. World's going to be a very unamusing place.

PRUE. Hardly likely, sir.

PARROTT. No end to which the prudes won't go.

Phone rings and he answers.

Parrott!

Listens. Then looks at PRUE.

Yes, she's here ... Sounds like something about a clinic.

PRUE. I'll take it outside.

PARROTT. No, no time for private calls, I want you here.

She takes the phone and talks sotto voce during the following:

NICK. So it isn't you that draws up this list?

TRIMMER. No. Our examiners.

NICK. And who would they be?

TRIMMER. Sound men, I assure you. One's been at it since the 1930s.

NICK. How's it affected him? Thirty-five years of filth?

PARROTT. Not one iota. A seagreen Incorruptible. Descended from Nelson's Commander-in-Chief at the Battle of Cape St Vincent.

NICK. Well-qualified then. Is he the one who thinks my play lacks grace, breadth of vision, power of utterance, common humanity?

TRIMMER. No, that's the ex-tutor to the daughter of the Governor of Bengal.

PARROTT. Just a minute! How do *you* know what he said? That's in his confidential report. Has there been a leak? I will not tolerate leaks in this office!

PRUE *puts down phone.*

Not for you, I hope, Miss Freebody? The clinic?

PRUE. No, sir, you misheard. The Garrick. For you. Confirming your abortion. Luncheon!

PARROTT. When's that?

PRUE. Today. One o'clock.

PARROTT. No. Didn't I tell you? Today I have a meeting. In the Libel Room of the London Readery.

His turn to be confused.

PRUE. The lying-in room of the London Breedery?

Hers again.

PARROTT. The Reading Room of the London Library!!

PRUE. Shall I cancel the Clinic? The Phallic?

PARROTT. The Garrick. Yes.

PRUE. I'll do it from my own desk.

She goes to A.

PARROTT. Where were we?

PRUE *opens A and in falls* JACK, *same age as* DENIS *and exactly like him, being played by the same actor, but wears a different uniform: Fleet Street 1960 – drainpipe trousers, Hush Puppies, short mac, Robin Hood hat. He'd been listening.*

PRUE. Who are you? And what are you doing there?

As he stands, she gives a little shriek. TRIMMER *sees too.*

PRUE *and* TRIMMER. Denis!

JACK. No. Jack.

PRUE. You look just like this – character – I knew once.

JACK. A guardsman?

PRUE. Yes.

JACK. My twin brother, Denis.

PRUE. That explains the remarkable resemblance.

RANDY (*aside*). Something has to, apart from keeping the cast down to seven.

DAPHNE (*entering at B*). Your trousers may be some time, sir. They're inundated with nether-garments down there. Overwhelmed. There's a pair from almost every office.

PARROTT. And whose fault's that? Seems to me you've been going through St James's Palace systematically dowsing Her Majesty's servants with Typhoo –

JACK. Now, now, my friend, out of order!

DAPHNE. Our Jack!

JACK. Morning, Mum.

DAPHNE. What you doing here?

JACK. A little bird told me our Denny's been a naughty boy.

DAPHNE. Our Denny? Never!

JACK. So I'm informed. Not been straight with Sandra. Been giving one to some bit of rough he's picked up –

PRUE *and* TRIMMER. I beg your pardon!

Then they're both confused as the others stare at them.

I mean – no, nothing ... disgusting expression, that's all I meant, et cetera.

JACK. Been giving him a fair amount of aggravation, by all accounts. So I come to face whoever-it-is with a bit of family solidarity ...

PRUE *and* TRIMMER *both keep their faces turned away from him.*

DAPHNE. We ought to stand together. Just as our Denny ought to give it a rest.

JACK. So you can't put a name to this old shagbag?

DAPHNE. I can guess, my son. Someone I could touch with a very short stick.

Her eye travels past TRIMMER *who's doubled up, studying the scripts, to* PRUE *who's hiding behind* PARROTT.

All la-de-da. Little Miss Cross-legs.

PARROTT. I don't know who you are or how you got in –

JACK. That's never a problem, squire. A fiver in the sergeant's pocket, he's not bothered. It's not exactly chock-a-block with nuclear warheads, is it?

PARROTT. Right. That's it. I've heard enough filth flung at my regiment for one day. (*Taking up phone.*) Hullo, Duty sarnt-major, please. Colonel Parrott speaking –

JACK. Who?

PARROTT. Sarnt-Major, we have an intruder who's slipped by and is impugning your honour as a non-commissioned officer/ of the crown –

JACK. Hello, squire. I'm Jack Meddler. Ring a bell?

PRUE *shuts the door and stays.*

You rang me with some story for my paper/ about some argie-bargie . . .

PARROTT. As you were, sarnt-major. False alarm.

Puts down phone. Speaks to JACK.

You've no business coming here. I said the Leaking Room of the Mundane Bribery.

JACK. You also said the Lord Chamberlain's a Russian spy.

PARROTT. Hell's teeth, d'you think I've gone doolally? No one in the Queen's Household, how dare you! No. Harold Wilson.

TRIMMER, DAPHNE, RANDY, PRUE *and* NICK. A Russian spy, the PM?

PARROTT. If you don't believe me, ask MI5, MI6, the CIA, the BBC, even the KGB –

TRIMMER. How's the BBC involved?

PARROTT. Are you serious? That daisy-chain of nancies and tosspots, rogering one another at the licence-payers' expense. Commies to a man, solely responsible in 1945 for spitting on the architect of victory/ in his finest hour –

JACK. Hang about, squire, I can't use all this, much as we'd like to. It's an official secret. A no-no. The PM's office would have/ my guts for garters.

PARROTT. Precisely. Just as when Wilson's arse-licker got wind we knew his boss was a Commie spy, he shunted me into this backwater, where I could do no further harm.

TRIMMER. Or good, sir.

PARROTT. Exactly, Bill. Well, right here in this leper colony, I've uncovered an even more sinister conspiracy. A plot involving some of the best-known names in the British theatre, every man jack of them taking public money from the Arts Council for a campaign of trendy-wendy left-wing slander.

TRIMMER. Yes, to show the powers-that-be with their pants down. Um. Sorry, sir.

RANDY. If only! I mean to say, this was a real chance to have a go at the establishment and you (*To* NICK.) chickened out.

NICK. What's a play lying in a drawer? An unborn baby. A twinkle in the author's eye. I want to see *Foreign Bodies* on the stage.

RANDY. Not that one. This one we're in. This Whitehall farce –

NICK. *A Game of Soldiers*? –

RANDY. – that should have faced up/ to the issue of freedom of expression.

NICK. How can I have written it when I'm in it? I wrote *Foreign Bodies*, yes –

PRUE. Weren't you in that as well?

JACK. And wasn't I, under another name?

They all protest that they're doubling parts. NICK *stands, cornered.*

TRIMMER. Go on. Duck and dodge. Wash your hands of it. He's as half-baked as his play. Why should an audience pay to see shows without heroes?

PRUE. As Isabel herself says: we look to our stars to take the whip-hand ... dominate us, wear the trousers. Sorry, sir, I didn't mean –

PARROTT. I've had enough of this. Give them back. At the double!

Goes to the wings and we glimpse backstage as he calls to an ASM who rushes for his trousers.

RANDY. Colin's a wanker. A member of the post-war generation that came to manhood just as his elders abandoned the Empire, right? Brought up to inherit the earth, then cut off with sod all.

DAPHNE. Language!

NICK. While Bernie, I suppose, is the new rising class of yobboes that will finally become yuppies/ and take over from your lot –

DAPHNE. Surely yuppies haven't been invented yet?

PARROTT (*returning with trousers, puts them on*). Go on. Blame the parents. And the uncle. But don't forget they saved the civilised world from barbarism. Not once but twice. Shell-shocked into silence and secrecy. That's how I see Uncle Lionel.

DAPHNE. And the poor mothers like Hester? Kept the home-fires burning, dug for victory, became secret drinkers, went quietly barmy. They're the ones should have got the medals. But all they did was shut their eyes and think of England.

PRUE. And young post-war women, before the Pill, expected to be virgins and tarts at the same time./ Trying to balance both –

DAPHNE. Darling, d'you mind?

PRUE *stops*.

I mean, you've been in this act from the start, while I've been stuck in the dressing-room listening to all of you on the speaker. Very nearly finished my nephew's jumper. You know I was in two minds about taking these parts, as Daphne was not much more than a spit and a cough in Act Two. Half an hour before she's seen at all, no sooner on than she's off again to fetch a biscuit. On again and it's off with the colonel's trousers. I mean off-stage. Then she stands here struck dumb while you all go whingeing on about the size of your parts. No, it's time I spoke. And, if I may say so, Nicholas dear, you've seriously undervalued the tea-lady's potential. She alone embodies the continuing strain of earthy humour in English life. From the Wife of Bath in Chaucer through, say, Juliet's nurse and Doll Tearsheet, down to Hogarth and Rowlandson, till the Victorians finally gagged her and forced her to resort to the prudery of *double entendres* ... at least while she's in the censor's office. And even here she's raised her husband's bawdry to an almost mythic level ... God, such potential there! I know your point is that bourgeois playwrights have turned her sort into the comic servant, as a way of keeping them in their place. But, darling, I have to say you've/ quite failed to articulate that particular –

NICK. No! Say no more. I've had enough. More than enough.

His sudden shout silences them all.

You expect me to stand here taking this? Everyone can slag off my play and I'm supposed to smile and say 'thanks'? How'd you like it if I told you how to play your parts? Or was always trying to put words into *your* mouths?

They look confusedly to one another but no one answers.

Better still, if I *stopped* putting them? Look at you. Dumbstruck. Speechless. Go on. Improvise. Make it up as you go along. Let's see how soon the seats start tipping up.

After some moments the actors start to speak, as themselves, apparently extempore.

RANDY. This isn't really fair, Nick.

NICK. Fair? Don't forget, I can do whatever I want with you. Whatever I want.

He tears the script in half and they freeze. NICK *fetches the typewriter, puts it on the coffee-table and starts writing.* DAPHNE *goes behind him, takes a phial from her pocket and pours poison into one of the cups, fills it with tea.*

JACK (*to* TRIMMER). Hang about! Don't I know your face? Didn't I meet you one time with our Denny?

TRIMMER (*quailing*). Me?

JACK. In that pub where the civil servants go cruising for their rough trade?

TRIMMER. Rough trade? Cruising?

JACK. And in the cottages? Nice bit of frottage in the cottage, eh? Or doing the 'dilly?

TRIMMER. What language is the fellow speaking?

JACK (*writes again*). 'Gay's the word in Censor's Love-Nest'.

TRIMMER. No comment. You'll be hearing from my lawyers.

He goes into the lavatory and shuts the door.

DAPHNE (*offering* NICK *the poisoned cup*). With all that brain-work, Mr Boswell, you could do with another cuppa. One sugar, was it?

NICK. Thank you, Daphne.

JACK. I think I've got the scoop I come for. The scandal in high places.

PARROTT. Nobody leaves this office who hasn't signed the Official Secrets Act.

JACK. This ain't the Bloody Tower. This is a free country. And I represent the free press.

He goes, door A. PARROTT *searches the desk-drawers.* NICK *types on.*

A cry and a thump from the lavatory. PRUE *says through the door:*

PRUE. You all right, Wing Commander?

PARROTT *finds his service revolver and loads it.*

PARROTT. It's got to be stopped.

JACK *reappears in the courtyard, crossing towards the main gate.* PARROTT *scribbles a note, leaves it and follows by A.*

PRUE. Mr Trimmer!

Opens the door to show TRIMMER *hanging by his old school tie from a hook in the ceiling.* PRUE *screams and collapses.* DAPHNE *attends to her.*

A shot offstage and JACK *falls out of sight.* PARROTT *follows with a smoking gun, stands over* JACK *as he dies.*

DAPHNE. Easy, love, relax ... you don't want to start it off too soon ... not here in the Palace.

RANDY *goes to look through window at* JACK, *then at* TRIMMER *then* PRUE, *then* NICK, *who has paused, lost for words.*

RANDY. You don't think you'll ever get away with this?

NICK. Good. Thanks.

RANDY. Thanks for what?

NICK *types.* RANDY *crosses to desk, reads the note.*

'It's time for the Roman way.'

PRUE. What?

RANDY. The colonel's note.

He opens the window and calls through to PARROTT.

You're playing into his hands.

Points at NICK, *still typing.*

DENIS, *the uniformed guardsman, having heard the shot, runs on, his rifle at the ready, bayonet fixed.*

DAPHNE. This one's having a miscarriage.

RANDY. I'll call an ambulance.

Starts to phone. As DENIS *holds his gun on guard,* PARROTT *runs on it, impaling himself. Falls.*

DAPHNE. Oh, my Gawd Almighty! Violence is no solution. Only leads to more and more death. More and more mothers grieving over their lost boys.

PRUE. Colonel ... my love ... my one and only ...

She crawls to touch his hand as it hangs through the window, breathes her last.

DAPHNE. She's gone too. Where will it end? (*Gasps and clutches her heart.*) One of my attacks. My pills.

RANDY (*supplying the cup she gave* NICK). Where?

DAPHNE. In my handbag, on the trolley.

But she dies of cardiac arrest before RANDY *can get to her with the pills and a cup of tea. He looks at* NICK, *who removes the page and scans it.* RANDY *tips the pills onto the floor and is about to sip the tea, looks at the cup, pauses and lowers it.*

NICK. Go on. Say the line.

RANDY. You don't think you'll ever get away with this? I turned down a Hollywood film to direct this play. No, not this castrated cadaver you've ended up with, the one you wrote.

NICK. Shut up and do as you're told. Drink the tea, like you drank the beer when you came to our house in Shrewsbury.

RANDY. I never went there. You made that up too. I never drank the poison. I never died. In real life Isabel married *me*.

Well, Virginia, if we're naming names. You're seriously confused, my friend.

NICK. Virginia and Randy.

RANDY. Ferdie.

NICK. Ferdie, yes. I read about you two when I go to the dentist. Darlings of the paparazzi. You've knocked her about in most of the world's best restaurants. The stretch limo, the pool, the world fame. That's not what she wanted.

RANDY. She's learnt to live with it. (*As* NICK *begins typing.*) Lies won't help you. But I reckon they're all you've got . . . half truths . . .

NICK. It's called fiction.

RANDY. It's called revenge. Making me out a sadistic pornographer and her a blue-movie star.

NICK. I did one version where she stayed with me and we lived happy ever after. Here.

He searches among his papers, spreading them on the floor.

RANDY. Five years later and still wanking?

NICK. Pirandello said: you either live life or you write it.

RANDY. Then he was a wanker too. I can't bear to look at this. So tacky. Like the live theatre itself. That's why the punters have stopped going. Who wants to watch live men and women doing embarrassing things? It's Voyeurism. They agree to play the game, to believe the actors are who they say they are, the room's got four walls, then you kick them in the crotch. 'No they aren't, no it hasn't.'

He turns parts of the set so that the Act One room returns.

It's finished, all this.

NICK. You got the girl, the Oscar . . . all right. But I at least had this.

He takes in the auditorium.

And now you want to destroy that too?

RANDY. It's *self*-destroyed. And – if you want to get this play on the stage – I should think twice about that ending.

NICK. I have, as you know. More than twice. Look!

Shows the various drafts of the play, now spread on the floor.

RANDY. And trash this one we just did. All those murders...

NICK. That was to remind you all I'm still in charge.

RANDY. For now. But one day we directors will get ours. You need us more than we need you. We've got two thousand years of *dead* playwrights to choose from. And those buggers don't come to rehearsals.

He's moved off the stage into the stalls and goes by an exit door. NICK *sits at his typewriter, the light reducing to a tiny pool. He reflects, speaking out front as though to the departed* RANDY.

NICK. Five years later, did you say? Twenty-five! I'm the wrong side of fifty and still remembering. This is the nineties. You'll love it, Ferdie ... Russia's down. America's up. The lunatics are running the asylum. And out in the world you call real it's blue murder ... but I want order ... limits. Sooner have a sort of tyranny to play hide-and-seek with ... what's a little injustice now and then? A few voices silenced?

He goes upstage and turns back the Act One screen.

Better be artful, duck and dodge. Better prune the garden than get lost in a jungle.

The other revolves turn as he goes back to the typewriter.

Give me a game with rules ... bendable rules ... like farce...

He likes the thought and types. Lights go on upstage and the others wake. PRUE *stands and goes to tidy the desk, etc.* PARROTT *stands,* DENIS *walks off,* TRIMMER *comes from the lavatory,* DAPHNE *gets up.*

DAPHNE. Elevenses? It's more like half-past-twelveses. I shall have to get my skates on. And I don't know what you're whingeing about, my son. The Lord Chamberlain only lasted another year. These days he just looks after the toilet-rolls. So you can say what you like.

NICK. No censors any more, just deaf ears.

DAPHNE (*to audience*). Never satisfied, some of them. Bit like my husband. I turned round to him and said 'I'm putting bromide in your tea, then perhaps I'll get a night's sleep' . . . and he turned round to me and he said . . .

She goes off by B as PARROTT *and the others enter.*

NICK. What's a little injustice now and then, a few voices silenced? Better be artful . . . duck and dodge, yes. Better prune the garden than get lost in a jungle.

PARROTT. Right! Prue, come along.

VIRGINIA *becomes* PRUE *and helps* TRIMMER.

And that's enough, that man! No more messages, thank you. You're not the post office. Don't forget what happened in the old days to messengers who brought bad news. (*Gestures slitting throat.*) Your job's to entertain, got that? You start telling people what to think, they'll think the opposite. It's a play, am I right?

NICK. Sah!

PARROTT. Stand easy, clear up that shambles and let's get on. Barely an hour before luncheon.

TRIMMER. And at fifteen hundred hours Sir Laurence Olivier's coming with our friend Kenneth T-T-T-Tynan.

PARROTT. Lordie! Again? They must like us. Where were we?

NICK *gathers his script and joins the others.*

NICK. You mean you might still give it a licence?

PARROTT. Don't see why not, with a little give-and-take.

NICK. Oh, I'll bend over backwards.

PARROTT. That won't be necessary, will it, Bill?

TRIMMER. Strictly disallowed.

They all laugh and settle to work.

PARROTT. Page, Miss Freebody?

PRUE. Twenty-five, Colonel.

TRIMMER. 'Somerset Maugham. He makes a decent screw.'

They all look at him.

NICK. Well?

PARROTT. Is that accompanied by a gesture?

NICK. Gesture?

PARROTT. Come along, Bill. Help me show him. Prue –

As they gather downstage to demonstrate, thunder, door-chimes, phone bells and fragments of 'Nice People' and the Schubert Impromptu come from the speakers. They all look at the prompt corner as the opening music returns.

Blackout.

Good authors too who once knew better words
Now only use four-letter words
Writing prose . . .
Anything Goes.

Lights up and the stage crew are completing the scene-change to Act One as the actors struggle through to take their calls.